RISE OF THE GIRL

Seven Empowering Conversations
to Have with Your Daughter

BY JO WIMBLE-GROVES

DK LONDON
Publishing Director Katie Cowan
Art Director Maxine Pedliham
Senior Acquisitions Editor Stephanie Milner
Managing Art Editor Bess Daly
Copy Editor Shari Last
Proofreader and Indexer Elizabeth Dowsett
Jacket Designer and Illustrator Holly Ovenden
Editor Kiron Gill
Designer Jordan Lambley
Photographer Francis Augusto
Stylist Alexandra Fullerton
Hair and Makeup Jo McKenna
Senior Production Editor Tony Phipps
Production Controller Rebecca Parton

First published in Great Britain in 2021 by
Dorling Kindersley Limited
DK, One Embassy Gardens, 8 Viaduct Gardens,
London, SW11 7BW

The authorised representative in the EEA is
Dorling Kindersley Verlag GmbH. Arnulfstr. 124,
80636 Munich, Germany

A CIP catalogue record for this book is available from the British Library.
ISBN: 978-0-2415-0684-4

Printed and bound in the United Kingdom

For the curious
www.dk.com

This book is a work of non-fiction based on
the life, experiences and recollections of
Jo Wimble-Groves. In some cases, names
of people and places have been changed
solely to protect the privacy of others.

This book was made with Forest
Stewardship Council ™ certified
paper – one small step in DK's
commitment to a sustainable
future. For more information go to
www.dk.com/our-green-pledge

RISE OF THE GIRL

Seven Empowering Conversations to Have with Your Daughter

BY JO WIMBLE-GROVES

"To be yourself in a world that is constantly trying to make you something else is the greatest accomplishment."
– Ralph Waldo Emerson

This book is for my daughter, Erin, and every girl around the world

CONTENTS

Children go through a lot of transformation in their early years. In this chapter, we research which changes in brain development take place at age seven, and whether they play a key role in how we develop socially.

A chapter about turning passions into possibilities. We look at ways we can help our girls find and nurture the subjects and hobbies they love.

1. "I don't like putting my hand up in class!"
We explore what might encourage girls to raise their hands, whether to answer a question at school or to try something new.

2. "I can't do this. Other people do this."
How people gain confidence through different experiences. We explore how to encourage girls to look at new things with wonder instead of fear.

3. "I really messed up today – what am I going to do?"
How we learn through failure and how we must help our girls realise it's the courage to continue that counts.

4. "I am rubbish at maths. Even my teacher thinks so!"
How we must reframe criticism. We can't let our girls' weaknesses shape their identities. We must teach them to celebrate their strengths instead.

5. "She's really awesome. I wish I could be more like her."
How to help our girls find strong, positive role models.
We should try to remember that everyone can be a role
model to someone else, often without even realising it.

6. "Why would she say that? I thought she was my friend."
Dealing with the frenemy. Teaching your daughter
how to handle the mean girls and showing her
what real friends look like.

7. "We lost another game. Maybe I should quit."
Fail again, try again. How we teach perseverance – and
how we can help our girls decide when is the right time
to try something else.

How to help our girls learn to believe in themselves
every day. Reminding them that, instead of dwelling
on their imperfections, they should focus on all the
great things they can do.

Life is never plain sailing and, for our girls, there
will inevitably be struggles along the way. But these
challenges can make us stronger. When our daughters
worry and feel afraid, we must guide them to break
through that fear barrier.

FOREWORD

Sarah Weller

Parenting consultant, coach
and certified NLP (neuro-linguistic
programming) practitioner

In this book, Jo Wimble-Groves is asking you to have seven conversations with your children. They will show you how you can encourage your daughters to celebrate who they are, and not be afraid to show that to the world.

Every day we are told, by ourselves and others, that we should be happy and positive. This goal translates to an agenda in our parenting that we must make our daughters happy in order for them to feel confident enough to build an independent and successful life. However, I believe that by making "happiness" our main parenting goal, we can miss opportunities to teach our children the skills that create sustainable success, in terms of how they feel about themselves, and what they choose to do in life in order to live independently. Sustainable success can only be created through a secure foundation of emotional regulation and resilience. Growing resilience is a more useful goal than pursuing happiness, because it will help our daughters find contentment in their internal and external worlds.

We know that the experience of assigning meaning to ourselves as individuals takes place around the age of two, when words start coming together to form sentences, at which point children are able to start naming things and experiences. By age four, children start to experience being seen as a unique person of significance.

Young children interpret what is told to them as fact and they begin to create a story about themselves, which they refine as they grow. It is at age seven that the child's self-defining story – known as an "inner script" – has been developed and internalised.

I believe that some of our parenting decisions, despite our positive intentions, can lead to a less-than-positive and less-than-confident inner script. Therefore, it's crucial for us as parents to consciously make our words, our communication, our conversations and our actions significant and intentional in order to build self-esteem through a positive parenting philosophy.

You may have heard of the psychologist Dr Carol Dweck, whose 1998 research paper suggests that "over praising" can undermine a child's motivation and performance. How we praise, how we discipline, how we ask for the behaviours we want to see, how we punish the behaviours we don't want to see, how we problem-solve – whether we try to "fix" things from a place of control or collaboration – all contribute to a child's development.

We want the focus to be on what our daughters can do, rather than what they think they can't do. In the early years, the emphasis should be on "being", rather than "doing".

Rise of the Girl is a current and relevant response to the global rise of girls and young women feeling anxious about finding their place in a world that is constantly changing: politically, economically, socially and environmentally. This anxiety can translate into the limiting belief that "less than perfect" can never be "good enough". This way of thinking can cripple a girl's motivation and curiosity. It can impede her ability to dream big.

In 2018, the Mental Health Foundation reported some data that was released by NHS Digital. Their aim was to shed some light on the mental health of our children and young people. The figures showed that for ages 17–19, nearly one in four young women had a mental health disorder, with emotional disorders (particularly anxiety) the most commonly reported.

The rise in teenage anxiety and depression could be tackled by something as simple as having the seven key conversations described in this book. Why are these seven conversations so important? Because when we strive for excellence, rather than perfection; when we reward and praise for effort, rather than ability; when we encourage curiosity for curiosity's sake; when we encourage experimentation; when we talk about the positive impacts of failure, we can reframe the developing mindsets of our daughters.

This book will help you reflect on, and have an honest conversation about, the role of fear in today's parenting approach – how fear seeps into what our daughters see, hear and experience from an early age. One of the key messages of this book is to reassess our relationship with failure. Failure in itself doesn't interfere with happiness if we are able to bounce back and accept that life is difficult. Using the concept of the growth mindset – that we must believe in our capacity for self-improvement – which is at the core of the seven conversations, we can teach our children to dare to be different, dare to dream, dare to make mistakes and dare to be curious.

Anxiety is the thief of dreams, of contentment and of resilience. Read on to discover ways to increase your daughter's chances of happiness.

INTRODUCTION

If I ask you to think about a strong and confident woman you know, who springs to mind? What do you think about when you look at that woman? What challenges did she face that eventually shaped her? What opportunities did she take, either in childhood or as an adult, that took her out of her comfort zone? Have you ever asked her?

Behind every confident woman is a story. A story that will reach back to her childhood and the experiences (both good and bad) that shaped her into the amazing woman she is today.

Strong women want their voices to be heard. I know those women, too, and I admire them. Seek out the strong women around you and talk to them about how they got to where they are now. Then encourage your daughter to talk to them too. Help our girls learn from them, so they can aspire to follow in their footsteps. Everyone has a story to tell, but how often do they tell it?

I want to start by sharing a story of my own. There is something quite magical about telling a story. Some say that storytelling unites people and creates deeper connections. I think it's also a powerful method for learning. Well, that's how I like to see it anyway.

It Starts with a Story

It was the summer of 2018, and I was at the height of my personal career. It was a mild, sunny day in the city of London. I love days like these. I got off the underground at Goodge Street station and enjoyed the short walk to the British Museum. I had never been to the British Museum before, despite it being one of the largest museums in the world. In fact, I had visited very few museums in my life. This trip would be a new experience for me.

On arrival, it took my breath away how beautiful this place was, inside and out. The much-loved listed building is rich in history and home to countless ancient objects. Although it's an old building, inside it's so modern. The iconic glass ceiling is quite a spectacle and it made me think about the concept of women smashing down glass ceilings. Gosh, how things have changed over the last 100 years. Perhaps that was why the British Museum had been chosen as the venue to host that year's STEM (science, technology, engineering and mathematics) Women's summer conference – the precise reason why I was there. I had been invited by the organisation STEM Women to deliver an inspiring keynote speech to more than 250 graduates. I was going to talk about how these bright girls are the future. A new wave of British entrepreneurs hidden within the architecture of this classic British building. I loved the idea of mixing old and new in perfect harmony within these walls. I was suddenly very aware that I was the old and they were the new…

I was welcomed with beaming smiles by the event conference team. As I walked down the stone staircase to the lecture theatre, I noticed that the graduates were buzzing and chatting while making their way to their seats for the next session. *My* session. So, without too much time to spare, I followed them into the theatre and made my way towards the stage and the largest television screen I had ever seen.

This would be the second-largest keynote I had delivered so far, and, as it was in the British Museum, it was sure to become a career highlight. Little old me in the British Museum, the most visited site in the UK. I thought about the people who had graced this stage before me. From brilliant professors to English rugby player Jonny Wilkinson and contemporary artist Grayson Perry. They have all presented on this wonderful stage. I suddenly realised how fortunate I was to have been asked to come here and deliver my talk.

I am rarely nervous before speaking, but somehow this one felt different. As I approached the lectern, the lights dimmed, and I was very aware of the hundreds of pairs of young, eager eyes on me. *Me.*

Being a woman in tech, this was an opportunity to talk about my favourite subject. I was about to deliver a great, motivational keynote on how the audience are the next generation of entrepreneurs – which was hugely exciting to me. So, with all the excitement bubbling in my chest, why did my hands feel clammy? Why was I nervous? I had delivered this keynote many times before, but somehow that day felt different. Maybe it was because I was in such a place of history. I felt more pressure than usual.

I started to talk. As I spoke about my career in tech, which started out for me at the age of just sixteen, I thought to myself, *I hope they find this interesting.* I shared a personal story about my daughter and how she had learnt to win through the power of failure. It's a story I love to share with those who are willing to hear it. I talked about the importance of "raising your hand" and why we must seize the opportunities that are in front of us despite being afraid. I spoke with passion, energy and ease. Ten minutes in and my keynote was rolling at a good pace – I had found my rhythm.

I glanced around the room, gesturing with my hands as I spoke into the microphone. Suddenly, I clocked one girl yawning. That didn't seem like a good sign. She hadn't even bothered to put her hand over her mouth to disguise it. I suppose it could have been worse. She could have been asleep.

I found myself panning around the room once more, just to check if anyone *had* fallen asleep. Fortunately, they hadn't. I tried not to feel offended, but I wondered if she found me uninspiring. Perhaps she thought my talk was boring? I wasn't sure. It was at that precise moment that Impostor Syndrome kicked in. That feeling when you imagine a huge, flashing neon arrow pointing down at your head, that says, "'What are *you* doing here in the British Museum?" Internally, I questioned myself.

What am I doing here?
Do I deserve to be here?

What is it that makes us feel like this? Impostor Syndrome, also known as Impostor Phenomenon, has been studied for more than three decades. That little annoying voice inside that tells you you're not *good enough*. It thrives on your self-criticism, so the more you talk to yourself in a negative way, the more you become trapped in an "impostor cycle".

Many of us feel awkward or struggle to shout about our successes. Even if it's a small victory, just something that's important to us personally, we shy away from wanting to make a fuss about it. It feels like there's a fine line between being arrogant and being proud, saying, "Look what I have achieved." Many of us don't want to shout about our successes. We find it hard to say, "Yes! This is who I am and look at what I have done," without feeling the need to somehow apologise for it or justify it by saying it must have been plain *luck*.

And that is exactly how I felt on the stage that day, afraid of saying, "Yes, this is what I have achieved," that I didn't fully deserve to be here. I had achieved so much in my life so far. I had come a long way from being a seven-year-old girl who often struggled at school and hid behind her sense of humour when she couldn't do her homework. A little girl who was often told her work wasn't good enough. That day at the conference was a *good* day. Those graduates had come to hear from me. This apparently confident, successful, award-winning writer and entrepreneur. Yes, me. But there I was, in a room full of bright, academic students, already overthinking that I wouldn't be able to do half of what they can. But then logic kicked in and I gently reminded myself that we are all bright in *different* ways.

My keynote lasted around forty minutes and the more I spoke, the more my confidence soared. I ended the talk with my favourite slide up on the big screen: a picture of an open book. I reminded my audience that everyone has a story.

"Today I was kindly asked to come and share mine," I said. "I hope that one day, some of you in the audience will come back to the British Museum and share your own stories. That you will stand in front of an audience here and pass down what you have learnt to the next generation. We must pass on what we have learnt because that is how we continue to get better and better at being our best selves."

Applause filled the room and I felt victorious. I threw aside the Impostor Syndrome for that. The clapping ended and the students started to leave. As I was busy packing away my bag, I was approached by one of the students, a graduate called Hanna. She told me that she had enjoyed my presentation and that she really related to the topic of Impostor Syndrome. How ironic that I had been feeling it, even when I was talking about it. She also said that she enjoyed hearing the story about my daughter and how we can all learn a lot through failure. She went on to tell me what she had studied and what she planned to do next. I felt so pleased that she had wanted to come and take the time to give me some feedback. Because, let's be honest, many of us thrive on feedback and praise. Particularly praise. It's always nice to be told by someone that you did a good job. It was at that moment that I thought to myself, *Yes Jo. You've done a very good thing today and you should be proud of yourself.* That little internal voice giving us positive messages. That was a stark reminder for me that we must champion our inner mentor more than our inner critic.

I know I cannot help every girl with her future or career prospects. I know that not everyone can come to events like these. I know many girls may never be afforded this opportunity. But, in situations like these, I do what I can to support the young women who sit in front of me.

Because I ask you this, what if, by sharing our stories, we could change the world? What if, by sharing stories, we could change how our girls feel about themselves – one girl at a time? It's a powerful idea but it just might be possible.

One Girl, One Future

When it came to writing this book, I was frequently asked the same question: "Why are you writing a book just for girls? Surely you should write a book for every child?" This question always clouded my judgement. Why *was* I writing a book just for girls? I always answer the question in the same way, which seems to satisfy the majority. I chose to write a book dedicated to girls because I believe there is a crisis among our teenage girls right now.

As parents, we play a vital role in helping our children navigate life's changes and challenges. So how do we help them build confidence? How do we encourage them to put up their hand and grab an opportunity? How do we get them to try something new and learn without being afraid of failure?

I'm not saying boys wouldn't benefit from this book. After all, I have two sons as well as a daughter. I care about their mental health and self-esteem just as much as my daughter's. However, my decision was to write this one first. Perhaps I will write a book for boys next! But for now, the focus is on girls.

The subject matter of this book is what keeps me up at night. I go into schools, colleges and universities on a regular basis, mostly to talk to girls. I stand in front of audiences of hundreds of students. These girls look carefree and happy on the outside, but I'm aware that so many teenage girls are struggling with mental health, confidence and body image. In 2017, the UK's National Health Service (NHS) revealed that young people are the unhappiest they've ever been. One in ten girls aged 14–17 are being referred for specialist mental-health support. It appears that it is mostly girls who are affected, and this is now being referred to as a crisis on a worldwide scale. In the UK, NHS data on child and adolescent mental health has revealed significant differences between genders: More than two-thirds of antidepressants prescribed to teenagers are for girls. Around 90 per cent of children admitted to hospital for eating disorders are girls. Hospitalisations due to self-harm involving girls have quadrupled since 2005. In the US, according to the CDC (Centers for Disease Control and Prevention), suicide rates among teenage girls reached a forty-year high in 2015. In many ways, I felt that not only was this book going to be helpful, it was necessary.

During the lockdown in the summer of 2020, I was asked to be the first speaker at a virtual festival for Girlguiding UK, a charity I have worked with on a number of occasions. Girlguiding focuses on adventure, fun and friendship to empower hundreds of thousands of girls to be their best and face the challenges of growing up today. I really enjoyed recording the motivational talk for these teen girls. However, during those challenging times, I found that I couldn't quite connect with the girls through the screen, as I can face-to-face. I've realised that spending time around teenage girls really helps open up just a small window into their lives, so I can see what's really happening for them.

Introduction

Back in 2017, I was asked to volunteer at a guide camp on behalf of Girlguiding UK. There were hundreds of girls there, all excited to spend a weekend away from home and meet new people. We had a lot of fun. I watched and supported the girls as they took part in numerous activities: circus skills, a climbing wall and archery. Many girls were trying these new skills for the first time, which was a joy to watch.

There was this one girl who caught my attention. She was away from home for the first time and, although guide camp was supposed to be a good experience, she felt alone, upset and anxious. I am no expert on how to manage these situations, but as a parent, I just took some time to sit with her and I let her talk to me when she wanted to. I asked about the things she enjoyed and tried to dig a little deeper to understand what gives her confidence. I will never know for sure if spending the afternoon with that girl helped her make the most of her time at camp. I will probably never see her again, but I do hope that I was able to help her that day.

Every year, Girlguiding UK releases a survey that asks for real opinions from more than 2,000 girls and young women in the UK aged 7–21. Bearing in mind that my aim in writing this book is to support our girls in growing their confidence and being their best selves, the results are extremely relevant. Around 80 per cent of girls and young women aged 11–21 have thought about changing their appearance; 55 per cent would change their appearance to feel more confident; 54 per cent would do it to feel better about themselves; 32 per cent would do it to feel more accepted and to fit in. And 46 per cent of girls and young women aged 11–21 say they fear people will criticise their body and, in the case of such an event, it can knock their confidence and stop them from wearing clothes they like.

We know that adolescence is such an important time of change for our teens. It is a crucial period for developing social and emotional habits that will last for life. Somewhere along the line, our girls can become an internal ball of anxiety. So why is this happening? A common cause, often given for this dire situation, is the negative effect of social media, especially in relation to body image and perfection issues. On top of that, loneliness is a real problem for teens today because many of the ways in which we communicate are digital, leaving less time for face-to-face interaction. While research has documented a link between social media and girls' body image issues, this does not tell the whole story of why girls' mental health is in crisis. Blaming social media isn't the answer; the picture is much, much bigger than that. The global struggle that girls face over confidence and mental health is an ever-changing and complex issue. We need to explore what's happening for girls right now. We have a duty to do something about this crisis. As a mother of a daughter, *I* have a duty to do something.

Rise of the Girl

This book is a practical one. A way to help support you in raising a kind, confident, resilient girl. The book is structured around seven conversations. Seven of the most common issues, frustrations or fears that our young girls voice to us as they are growing up and finding their place in the world. I thought about what conversations were happening in my own home, with my daughter, Erin. I witnessed how she would sometimes throw her pencil across the room in frustration and announce that she felt she wasn't good at anything. It made me wonder how many other parents out there were experiencing similar situations and, more importantly, how we could reframe these negative conversations. I wanted to explore how to encourage girls to focus on their strengths, to raise their hands without being afraid, to try something new without fear of failure and to realise they could gain confidence by stepping out of their comfort zone.

In addition to the seven conversations, which can be found in chapter 3, *Rise of the Girl* covers other important areas of how we are developing our girls of today and tomorrow. Chapter 1 looks at the transformation in brain development that takes place at the age of seven, and how that plays a key role in shaping personality. In chapter 2, I explore how girls can turn their passions into possibilities. By encouraging them to pursue subjects and hobbies they love, we can help them grow their self-confidence. Chapter 4 reflects on the importance of self-belief. As Nirmal "Nimsdai" Purja says, "You can do anything you set your mind to, but it takes courage, belief and truth in yourself." As someone who broke records climbing the fourteen highest mountains in the world in less than seven months, I'm inclined to believe him. Aren't you? In chapter 5, I cover the topic of resilience, a key quality our girls will need in order to achieve their goals in this challenging world. We must help girls learn how to bounce back from the hurdles they will face along their journey and teach them that strength comes from getting through our failures.

The importance of role models and mentors for girls is crucial in helping them find their inner power.

At the end of each chapter, I include some practical tips or conversation starters that you can use in your everyday life with your amazing girl. I want this book to offer you advice and guidance in supporting your daughter, or a girl you know. Together we can raise our girls to listen to their inner mentor instead of their inner critic. My aim is to help you find the tools you need to help your girls on their journey to finding their best selves.

As parents and caregivers, we are often our girls' first role models. Role models are so important, and, with that in mind, I asked a number of successful, inspiring personalities to share their stories with us, either tales of their own experiences or lessons they have learnt from raising girls. Throughout the book, we will hear from a variety of contributors, including Anna Whitehouse (Mother Pukka), Nimsdai Purja, Molly Gunn (Selfish Mother), Steve Backley and Michelle Griffith-Robinson, to name just a few. These incredible individuals share their stories of strength and overcoming adversity, which I believe will be hugely inspiring for you to share with your own daughter.

The importance of role models and mentors for girls is crucial in helping them find their inner power. There is no question that mothers are a powerful influence on our girls. However, dads and other adults can also be hugely influential, and this should not be underestimated. This is a key reason why I felt strongly about including both men and women as contributors within this book. I wanted to hear different perspectives. From those who have daughters and even from those who don't. I love that my contributors have such varied methods of parenting or pathways to success that they are happy to share. Their fascinating stories add real-life experience from diverse points of view, enabling us to empower our girls to face the challenges of childhood and prepare them for an amazing adulthood – as tomorrow's dreamers, doers and entrepreneurs.

There is no magic formula to raising strong, confident girls. I wish there were. However, there is something uniquely powerful about using our voices to share what we know. There is strength in us coming together to guide our girls through all sorts of challenges. The road, even for myself as a mother of a daughter, still has a long way to be travelled. It is hard to navigate, but we walk this path together, building each other up along the way.

I've changed so much in the last eleven years, particularly since giving birth to my daughter, Erin. I'm so much more confident and have spent time getting to know myself a little better. I appreciate that "getting to know myself" may sound odd, but it's true. And so much of that change happened because I had a daughter. Having Erin gave me an overwhelming feeling that I needed to be a strong woman for her. A leader, a teacher, a mentor and a role model, for her.

So, if you're raising a girl or know a girl who needs your guidance, I have good news. I'm excited for their futures. Never before have more girls and women been busy making history. We have more female role models today, in just about every public sphere you can think of.

Sometimes, I think that what I do, going into schools to deliver talks, seems small and insufficient – but it's not. How powerful is it to go into a school and face a room of 100 girls? What if I could change just one girl's perception of herself? What if I can improve that one girl's self-confidence and make a difference to how she thinks about her future?

I want to be part of giving our girls the future they deserve. I want to be one of those people who is passionate about helping parents and caregivers of girls. In this book, I want to help your daughter – with your support – to thrive. So I am sharing what I have learnt. From being a sixth-form college dropout, to having a senior career in tech without a degree, through a decade spent delivering talks to secondary schoolgirls, and finally, simply as a mother of a daughter.

I am excited that you are reading this book; it means you're just as passionate about supporting girls as I am. Together, we can give them the tools they need to embrace a strong sense of self, which will steer them through adolescence. In this book, you will read incredible stories from contributors about how wonderful things came about from simply dipping their toes in the water, from trying something new.

Give your girl the opportunity to explore her interests. If she's a girly girl, that doesn't mean she won't enjoy cricket or football. If she's quiet, that doesn't mean she might not thrive at a drama class. Don't just sign her up for an extracurricular activity because it's popular. Where appropriate, go against the norm. Seek out different options and see what she chooses. I hope this book will make us consider whether our girls should do the things they are good at or the things they love. Perhaps it's about trying to find a balance of both.

Sometimes I get asked what legacy I want to leave behind, and it makes me think about what I am striving for. I want to be remembered as the person who worked to make a difference. I want to be remembered as someone who tried to help and support others. I want to be remembered as the person who lifted other girls up to help them become the success stories of tomorrow. We are the ones who should tell them they can achieve, even if they don't quite believe it themselves.

Raising girls is a learning process. Let's do it together. Let's go on a journey of trying new things, winning and losing, because that's how we build our self-confidence. Now is the time for our girls to shine. Now is the time for the rise of the girl.

And so, referring back to my very first question – why am I writing a book just for girls? – here is my answer: Never before have girls needed to raise their hands as much as now, and never before have there been so many opportunities available to our girls – if they will only reach up and grab them. Show your girl how to stand a little taller. Help her find her voice. Explain how positivity grows when we lift each other up. This is true empowerment, and this is how we should aspire to raise the girls of today and tomorrow. My ambitions started small, helping one girl at a time, so what impact might a book have?

Now is the time for our girls to shine. Now is the time for the rise of the girl.

Chapter 1

SEVEN

Children go through a lot of transformation in their early years. In this chapter, we research which changes in brain development take place at age seven and whether they play a key role in how we develop socially.

The childhood journey is an inquisitive, exciting and emotional one. Truth be told, I'd never really noticed all the "baby milestones" too much. I remember my daughter taking her first steps in our living room just after we had moved into our new home, but so much of those early years are hazy – even though I promised myself that I would remember. I convinced myself that I didn't need to write those sorts of things down because they were such great memories; of *course* I wouldn't forget what her two imaginary friends were called. But, frustratingly, I have forgotten. As has she. Perhaps it was the tiredness, which I'm not sure gets any better over time (apologies if you have a baby at home with you while you read this).

When parents with babies ask me if it gets easier, I always think that is such a tough question. Of course, we all want to be reassured that being up all night with the baby will pass, and yes, of course, in most cases, it does. (Apart from the case of my friend Caroline, who often reminds me that she didn't get much sleep for about three years!) However, I have learnt that it's not really a case of getting easier, but more that every phase is *different*.

Once the sleep returns, it's other things that keep you up at night instead. Watching your daughter get upset and frustrated when she finds her homework too challenging. Seeing her emotionally drained when certain friendships become fractured. We have entered a different phase of my daughter's journey through childhood. Time has slipped past in the blink of an eye, and developmental leaps have galloped past us. She is busy trying to grow up and go faster. I am trying hard to remind her to slow down and enjoy the moment. Now, my young girl is almost twelve and on the cusp of teenhood. Where has my baby girl gone? Every parent who has spent years and years raising children will tell you that it goes by "in a flash". We never believe them. But now I think they were right all along.

I want to tell you about my daughter when she was seven. Seven is a good age. I remember trying to help her with certain tasks at home, but she swiftly reminded me that she was *perfectly* capable of doing them herself. I tried to straighten her wonky ponytail once, but she told me that it's just *fine* just the way she had done it. "Mum, stop fussing."

In that moment, I had a seven-year-old standing in front of me. One who sits a little taller in her chair, her legs no longer dangling under the seat, swishing backwards and forwards like they used to. A girl who likes to own the TV remote control (and regularly hides it from her brother) – a constant frustration in our house! But most of all, I cherish the pure beauty and innocence of seven. A daughter who spends hours, perhaps days, imagining what a cross between a unicorn and a pug would actually be like to own *in real life*.

Being seven brings plenty of moments of happiness, tears and exuberance, but generally turning seven brings a little calm and quiet after the tussles and tangles of six, much to the relief of parents, caregivers and teachers. Seven-year-olds read, talk things over and try to work things out for themselves. But seven-year-olds can also be easily disappointed. Especially when things (as so often happens) do not turn out the way they expected. At home, I noticed how our daughter rushed to her room and slammed the door when things didn't go her way. You might think you have suddenly gained a teenager.

At age seven, emotions run high, but there is a good reason for that. Some of the most significant changes in the brain occur at this age, and these changes can shape a person – how we think and how we feel. The brain's frontal and temporal lobes, which control cognitive functions, grow *enormously* at this age. According to medical research, they grow more at seven than at any other time in a person's life. At the same time, these lobes are making neural connections with the system that controls emotions. In other words, both thinking and feeling get a major overhaul.

Lucky Number Seven

We are regularly told that the early years of childhood are so important. It's something I've spoken about many times with my mother-in-law, Madalene Wimble, a psychodynamic relationship therapist. In the twenty years we've known each other, Madalene and I have spoken at length about the importance of childhood. Madalene really helped me understand how the early developmental years play a pivotal role in helping children feel their emotions and build connections with others.

In a world that's
reliant on social
connectivity,
how our children
interact with others
can be central to
their happiness
and wellbeing.

I see seven as a magical milestone, and studies show that this age is important in your child's development of social skills. As adults, we know that social skills play a huge part in how we live. Being aware of other people's emotions, knowing when to listen and when to speak – these things can make all the difference in our interactions. In a world that's reliant on social connectivity, how our children interact with others can be central to their happiness and wellbeing.

If you have a seven-year-old, then consider yourself lucky. It's such a wonderful age, and they are hungry for learning and life. As parents, it can be a busy time, when your daughter might start extra activities and clubs, which are great. However, equally, this is a time when your daughter's brain needs to filter and adjust. I've seen that in my own daughter, and we had to scale back on some of the activities she was doing. Let's just say, it was all just getting a fraction too much and we have since taken our foot off the pedal. My husband and I worked together to realise and recognise that she only needed to do a few extra activities to boost her confidence.

As a parent, you may notice that things just seem to "click" for your seven-year-old. You may find that, ever so slowly, she is gently adjusting and establishing who she *is*. When we start to think about how we are going to raise a confident girl, we need to understand the importance of seven, and why what they learn at this age can have such an impact on their future social skills.

Researching the subject, I came across several medical reports that talk about the changes in the brain at age seven. As I mentioned earlier, cognitive functions grow and begin connecting with the brain system that controls emotions.

Let's look at some of the key milestones your child is likely to go through at seven. These are grouped into five categories: physical growth, cognitive development, emotional and social development, language development, and sensory and motor development. Remember, your daughter will grow at her own pace and we should take care to acknowledge that healthy growth is different for every child.

Seven-year-olds are inquisitive and curious, and they love to ask lots of questions! They suddenly feel mature enough to question things, but they still look to peers and other adults for reassurance of their own ideas.

At seven, your daughter will begin to show a preference for learning styles. For example, some children like hands-on activities, such as science experiments, whereas others like to work quietly and independently, such as by practising their writing, and others might enjoy using objects to tackle challenges, such as using counting beads to solve maths problems.

From an emotional development perspective, children of seven start to become more aware of and sensitive to the feelings of others, a trait we know as empathy. In his book, *Raising Girls,* psychologist Steve Biddulph states that girl babies have more awareness of social connection, because it is a natural strength of girls. He advises parents to continue to nurture this strength beyond their daughter's early years.

Your daughter is also starting to learn how to value herself. She's beginning to validate her own feelings and is learning about the importance of kindness, empathy and honesty – all crucial social skills to take her from childhood into adulthood.

Seven-year-olds start to form long-lasting friendships, and they enjoy playing in larger groups. Equally, at this age, you might notice your child needs some time alone.

Your seven-year-old has already started to shift her attention to people and pursuits outside of the family. This could be the turning point – when they really start to build on their natural social skills. It is also when role models start to come into play. Your daughter might start to get attached to adult influencers: a family member, a teacher or perhaps a friend's parent. These influencers could be instrumental in helping our girls find their sparks and identify their interests, a subject we will explore further in chapter 2.

When I was younger, I was really passionate about sport. My father used to coach our local football team, so I grew up in a sporty household and I enjoyed all kinds of sports, from netball and basketball to lacrosse and tennis. Sport can be a brilliant way for girls to develop their social skills and build new friendships. Thinking back, I don't recall seeing many female role models in sport, either in magazines or on the television. Nowadays, we see lots of incredible female role models, but there is still more work to be done to raise the visibility of successful sportswomen in the media. There's a phrase I like: "If you can't see them, you can't be them." Seven-year-old girls need to *see* these role models – there is no time to lose.

I have written *Rise of the Girl* to explore what girls are feeling right now. We know that girls are facing so many different pressures, from social to academic. However, the good news is that by talking about it, we have the ability to help our girls. To reach out our hands, guide them and ask them, "What do you need from us?"

There has never been a more important time to feel connected with our girls. If there is one thing we know for sure, it's that by providing structure and support for your daughter, you're giving her one of the most important sources of protection in her life. If we can build strong foundations for our girls, then, in turn, we hope they will have an easier time at school, in the workplace and in relationships. With that in mind, I spoke to two different experts: Madalene Wimble, a psychodynamic relationship therapist, and Dr Helen Woolnough, a research fellow in women's leadership. I don't claim to have all the answers in this book, but both of these women share some really important insights on what they think girls need. As mothers of daughters themselves, their words of wisdom are incredibly valuable.

In the many conversations I've had with Madalene Wimble, my mother-in-law, I have always found her insight so brilliant, and she helps me understand things in a really relatable way. During our discussions, I remember saying, "I wish I could write this all down! It would be so helpful to others." I'm so pleased that she has kindly agreed to contribute to this book, and I can now share some of her professional thoughts with you.

I first approached Madalene asking for her thoughts about parents or caregivers as a child's first role models. How can this positively or negatively influence a child's early years? And why is supporting girls through managing their emotions so crucial? Madalene is an experienced, fully qualified counsellor with a psychodynamic approach. Here, she shares her professional knowledge with us to help us understand the child inside:

The Child Inside
by Madalene Wimble

As children, so much within us comes from our initial caregivers. They are role models we see every day. This starts from the day you are born.

If you look into the eyes of a newborn baby, you will realise they will always, always be seeking out eye contact. A baby will look intensely into their caregivers' eyes, and, to them, they are "as one" with the parent. In this very early development stage, a baby does not experience its mother as being separate from her. Babies are born almost like a blank slate: they know nothing apart from when they're hungry, tired or hurting.

In these very early months and years, the baby's foundations are built. The baby will feel a parent's emotions very strongly. If you're upset, happy or anxious, babies will mirror these emotions right from the earliest days and can continue to feel them their whole life. An anxious, depressed mum will likely result in an anxious baby, as she will not have experienced the calm, soothing voice that makes her feel safe and nurtured. As the baby grows up, she may feel it is up to her to look out for and take care of the parent's feelings. She may even feel it's her responsibility to make the parent feel better, therefore she parents the caregiver, never fully experiencing what it's like to be truly parented and nurtured herself.

These very early feelings can remain with the baby throughout her life, and although we classify this sort of emotional behaviour under the general concept of "mirroring", actually, what happens is not just mirroring

— it's deeper than that: the baby or toddler fully internalises the caregiver's emotions and actions, as if they were their own.

There is a fine line when it comes to raising children. Although you may desire that your child should be a high-achiever, confident and self-praising, a critical parent may raise a child with an inner voice that critiques herself and others.

If our early development is not built on the right foundations, then, as the child grows, they will be without a voice of their own. Raising children is all about checking in with them, getting them to share their feelings and understanding them. This is what will give our children the confidence to find their true inner voice. And as we raise teens, it is so important to encourage and listen to their true inner voice.

Within my psychotherapy practice, my clients are adults, but we all carry the inner child within us, even through adulthood. I look at my work as helping the child within each of my clients. Over time, as my clients begin to discover their inner child, a picture starts to emerge and they are able to understand themselves more. I help them learn how to nurture themselves and make changes. Gradually, they begin to break things down and they will often realise they are not thinking, feeling or expressing through their own voice. As young children, we internalise our parents' voices, so if we had a negative experience of childhood, our adulthood can be influenced by this.

I will say to a client, "Let's look at those voices that don't come from your true self, but which belong to others. Let's take them out and put them to the side." It is so important we learn to listen to our own voice and not those we have internalised from others. I offer my clients a safe, non-judgemental environment where they feel happy enough to explore. It may be that, for the first time, they are able to voice how they truly feel, without believing it's wrong. It is so crucial to be able to do this. We all have a child inside of us and if that child has never been allowed to express its own thoughts and feelings, then it doesn't have a voice of its own.

Each child is different, and each child will experience things differently. Each child will internalise differently, but at the end of the day, each child will internalise.

As parents, we have internalised our own parents' voices too. We need to ensure that we are displaying positive behaviours to our children. Parents and caregivers are at the heart of every child. We need to catch our own behaviours early on, so we can raise our children the best way possible.

For some adults, their inner voice will be shaky, because they haven't ever had the opportunity to let it speak. In the work I do, I bring people's unconsciousness into consciousness. As soon as we are aware of our unconscious voices, we have the ability to make changes.

Mirroring happens on so many different levels, from how a child plays, to imitating Dad's deep voice, to the foods we eat, and so much more. However, a deeper form of mirroring is this internalising of emotion, and this will last a lifetime. As parents, we can learn from our children too. Parents and children need each other.

In my early thirties, I had my own counselling. When I started training to become a counsellor, my therapists became my role models. My journey of counselling started

"Listen to what
your child has
to say – always."

MADALENE WIMBLE

at a time when it was very taboo to go and see a counsellor. Having had therapy myself, and then going on to train over the course of twenty years, has helped me grow in a way I never would have done otherwise.

I was a young parent myself, just nineteen when I had my first baby, and I was not equipped with the skills to be a parent. I made mistakes. I got so much wrong, but I was prepared to take a risk and reach out to learn myself. At a later stage, I learnt to connect with my children because I got the help I needed and learnt how to be the parent my children needed me to be. Connecting with people feeds you as a human. Connections give you a sense of being, and children thrive from good connections. A good role model and a good parent will be someone that can really connect with a child, on that different level.

These are my top three things to remember on how to connect with your child:

Listen to what your child has to say – always.

Withstand their emotions. Let them feel their emotions, and validate them. Stand firm and be the parent.

Remember, there's no right or wrong in parenting. As long as you do your best to connect with your child and help them listen to their inner voice, then you are enough as you are.

We need to normalise talking about feelings. It's never too late to listen to your child. Respect them, and value them for what they say. A child, no matter what age, needs to feel safe enough that they can tell you how they feel, or how they have felt. As a parent it's important to take responsibility for helping your child find their own voice. I know that my children know the channels are still open to talk to me.

It is through life's experiences that you find your sense of self. We learn from each experience, and as much as you can say to your child, "You're good at this," the only thing that will really show them that, is time. As parents, all we can do is be there for our children. Whatever their future holds, support them in finding who they are. They may not always make the right choices, but it is through their wrong choices that they will learn.

I am very much one for positivity, but life isn't always positive. It is important for children to see that things go wrong. As a parent we can support them in getting back up, dusting themselves off and finding another way.

We know that parenting is complex. We often look to others to ask if we're doing it right, but when it comes to raising our children in the best way, the answers aren't always black and white. Madalene's insight has really enabled us to understand how important it is to nurture our children and help them learn to validate their own emotions, especially in those formative years leading up to age seven. It is clear that role models play a pivotal role in helping children navigate their feelings, and we should impress on our children that showing emotion can be a sign of strength rather than weakness.

Madalene's professional knowledge has shown us that creating a safe environment for our children from the start is essential. Giving children love and attention from the beginning could determine their wellbeing all the way into adulthood. So while the first seven years of life might not mean everything, I think we can feel confident that the first seven years play a major part in your daughter's developing social skills.

Knowing how crucial the early connections are and that they can influence so much that happens in later life, I started to think about how we can connect the dots between what we see in our seven-year-olds and what we see in young women as they move out of the safe sphere of school to enter further education or the workplace. Could those social skills we learnt at an early age still affect our adult interactions? Whether meeting new people or embarking on that first day at college or university, how a person carries themselves and makes connections from the start is vitally important. If we raise our hands from the age of seven, are we more likely to raise our hands in later life, when that much-wanted promotion presents itself? Could this all be connected with how the next generation of female leaders rises up to take opportunities?

In an article published in the *Harvard Business Review* in 2014, a shocking statistic was revealed: When going for a promotion, men put their hand up and applied for the job even when they met only 60 per cent of the required qualifications, whereas women applied only if they met 100 per cent of them. As one *Forbes* article put it, "Men are confident about their ability at 60 per cent, but women don't feel confident until they've checked off each item on the list." Girls need to feel confident to raise their hands and put themselves forward from a young age, without the fear of breaking the rules, or the fear of failure and rejection.

I thought about this a lot after speaking at an event for Warburtons in the UK some years ago. At the event, I listened intently to a keynote from Dr Helen Woolnough,

PhD, an associate fellow for the British Psychological Society. I spoke openly to Helen about my aspirations to write this book. (I was not even remotely close to getting a publishing deal at the time.) I asked her if she would be willing to share her thoughts in my book on the messages girls are given from a young age and what responsibilities we have, as parents, to share the right messages. Amazingly, she agreed straight away (and I was so grateful). Helen is a mother and a doctor of philosophy, so I knew she would offer an insightful view into gender stereotypes that exist from a young age, and that it would be very interesting to read about what hopes she has for her own daughter.

Helping Girls Thrive and Achieve
by Dr Helen Woolnough, PhD

As a doctor of philosophy and mother to a wonderful daughter (and an equally wonderful son), I recognise the challenges my daughter faces now – and may face in years to come. From the research I do at Manchester Metropolitan University addressing the challenges many women face in the workplace compared to their male counterparts, I know that both culture and social structures are at work to restrict women from navigating career pathways and fulfilling their career potential.

Whilst women and men have equal leadership potential, women occupy fewer, and less powerful, leadership roles than men. Figures from the Office for National Statistics show that the gender pay gap widened over three consecutive years, leading to a pay gap between male and female graduates in the UK of 17.9 per cent in 2019. Furthermore, one in twenty women are likely to be made redundant because they are pregnant or on maternity leave. I don't want my daughter (or indeed yours) to work hard all through school and university, just so they can spend decades being paid less than their male counterparts and potentially face further discrimination when (or if) they become mothers.

The statistics paint a pretty depressing picture, but there are many bright notes to celebrate, particularly those strong female role models who have synchronised successful careers with their family lives. Ours is a world of huge possibility, and I believe in playing my part to create a legacy that means my daughter will have a fairer chance in life. I want my daughter to understand that she is not the problem. She does not need to be "fixed" to fit in with the dominant (masculine) status quo, and she should not need to supra-perform to survive and progress. It's vital that girls hear this message loud and clear. Inequality persists because our daughters are faced with traversing a gendered landscape, which is often considerably less favourable to them than men. To secure real, lasting change, we need to work together to call out and challenge underlying gendered stereotypes and structures, which are harmful for girls as well as boys.

From childhood, young girls are given messages about the kinds of jobs they should and shouldn't pursue (e.g. not IT, engineering, construction), and how they should behave (e.g. not authoritatively or assertively because that can be interpreted as "bossy"). A UK survey by Education for Employers, which explored the career aspirations of children aged 7–11, found that more than four times the number of boys wanted to become engineers compared to girls, and nearly double the number of boys wanted to become scientists. This subject segregation at school and, following on from this, occupational segregation in the workplace, is one of the key contributing factors to the gender pay gap. Neuroscience has challenged the ingrained societal stereotype that girls and boys have different interests and are better at certain subjects than others because "that's just the way they're built". Instead, scholars recognise that expectations and behaviour are strongly shaped by socialisation, which perpetuates differences in self-confidence and risk-taking that drive boys and girls down different career trajectories.

As a parent, it's really difficult to buck these gender expectations, particularly when children are exposed daily to entrenched gender stereotypes from the media and in their interactions with others, but there is also great value in doing so for future female (and male) generations. There is no magic formula for this, but awareness, communication and education are crucial. Thinking back to when my daughter was seven years old, I remember a time when she had been learning about different artists at school and the colours and shapes that they used in their work (as well as coming home from school covered in paint a lot!) One day, as she was regaling me with tales of her latest artwork, she suddenly stopped, looked up at me rather perplexed, and said, "Mummy, why are there no female artists?"

In that moment I was disheartened to realise that she had only been exposed to male experts in the field, but I was also super proud of the fact she'd noticed! It opened up a dialogue about the value of girls and boys in all jobs and pursuits. (And – not being at all knowledgeable about the *world of art – a quick search on Google enabled me to find some trailblazing female artists and highlight my point!)*

An appreciation of how differences emerge can help end the gender divide. I want to prepare my daughter for a future I hope she will thrive in, and that means striving to raise a confident girl, free to realise her fullest potential. I hope that she will be bold and find resilience through cultivating a strong network of positive and supportive people around her. Ultimately, I just want her to know that she can.

————

Both Madalene and Helen have shown that self-belief can be instilled at a young age and continues to grow over time. It is so important to start helping your daughter believe in herself from a young age. Even by the age of seven, she will have internalised so many outside influences and cultural stereotypes, which is why we must make a big effort to ensure she can fulfil her potential whatever the outside world "tells" her.

Madalene reminds us that we must commit to growing a child's social and emotional skills throughout their childhood, and how not addressing this can affect their ongoing mental health. Ensuring these social and emotional foundations are built by the age of seven is hugely important. With the rise of social media, and with younger girls having access to platforms such as YouTube, some girls may see things online they are not ready to see. This type of activity can happen purely by accident. However, girls need to be comfortable to talk about what they see. We must give them the space to talk to us openly. Perhaps there has never been a more critical time to protect the mental wellbeing of the ones we love.

Helen's fascinating insights remind us that career aspirations and stereotypes can become ingrained by age seven. Her suggestion to make sure your daughter is aware of any imbalances is a really useful first step in addressing the negative stereotypes. From her research at Manchester Metropolitan University, Helen reinforces that we have to show our girls, from a young age, that careers don't need to be defined by gender. Smashing stereotypes needs to start from the get-go.

Let's raise our girls to be their own cheerleaders, leaders of their own futures, without being told what they can or cannot do just because they are girls. Different people naturally have different abilities and talents, and when it comes to equality, everyone should have equal opportunities to prove their talents and skills.

Encourage Her to be Her Own Cheerleader

Encourage her to come out of her comfort zone. We want to instil confidence in our daughters so they have the courage to step beyond what feels comfortable. Encourage your daughter to move past what she does well and tackle something different. Risk looks different to every girl – for your daughter it might look like joining the football team, reading in front of classmates or trying that new dance class when she doesn't know anyone. In the case of my daughter, Erin, she came out of her comfort zone to join a rugby team that had very few girls. However, playing in a boy-heavy team has helped her understand that, firstly, she's just as good as them, and, secondly, the experience of feeling different has made her feel stronger and braver. By sticking it out and playing well, she has earned the utmost respect of everyone in her team.

I understand that not every child is the same, so it's crucial to understand why your child doesn't feel comfortable to try something new. Maybe they worry they won't be good enough, or they worry about being liked. However, in my opinion, I think it's great to give things a go. Encourage your daughter to try a new activity. Perhaps suggest she does it with a friend or a cousin? Whatever the outcome – whether they enjoyed it, liked parts of it, found it wasn't as bad as they thought or really didn't enjoy it – discovering how they feel about it can be the best lesson of all.

Explain to her how failure is part of winning. Failure will happen, but how we deal with it is what's most important. It's inevitable, especially when your child is taking risks. It's also essential for her to learn to move through it, normalise it and rebound. Ask about how she sees her situation and help her talk it through. Then plan and agree on the next positive steps you can take together.

Learning from failure allows her to move forward, rather than retreat. Failure will happen at different stages of our lives and, as we get older, we understand that this is all part of the journey. If we, as parents, focus on getting things perfectly right all the time, then we have set our daughters up for failure already.

One of the NBA's (National Basketball Association) most famous and talented basketball players of all time, Michael Jordan, failed countless times. As he has admitted publicly, he missed thousands of shots and lost hundreds of games. However, he realised that's part of the process, so he used it as a driving force to work even harder. He emphasises that it was partly failure that enabled him to achieve huge success. Jordan's attitude is something everyone should admire. When you fail repeatedly, be aware that you're just getting closer to a triumph.

Niklas Hed, together with his mobile game development team, created fifty-one games – and all of them were failures. Hed went on to build Angry Birds, an app that dominated the app store for months, becoming a worldwide phenomenon. Countless failures might not seem like the secret to success. Some might say that creating fifty-one unsuccessful games is the very definition of failure. But it turned out to be only temporary. Rovio, Hed's Finnish company that was behind Angry Birds, has been valued at around $1 billion. I think we can define that as a success?

Show your daughter how to believe in herself. This may sound like a cliché, but from the age of seven, show her that believing in herself is important. Some may say that it's background, connections or luck that create successful people, but I would say that mindset and self-belief play a huge part in a person's success. Although many factors influence the pathway to success, in my view, the biggest contributing factor to achieving something significant is self-belief. Without this key ingredient, many of us can't thrive personally or professionally.

Seven Conversation Starters to Ask Your Daughter in Seven Days

Is your daughter quiet when she comes out of school? Do you only get one-word answers when you try to ask her about her day? Here are some alternative questions to try, which are aimed at seven- to twelve-year-olds but can be adapted where necessary. Hopefully, these conversation starters will help your daughter open up to you.

1. **What do you enjoy most about school?**

2. **Tell me three things you feel you are good at.**

3. **What makes you feel good about yourself?**

4. **What hobbies do you enjoy? What makes you happy?**

5. **Did anyone make you feel sad today?**

6. **Is there anything you want to talk about?**

7. **What are you grateful for today?**

Chapter 2

FINDING THEMSELVES

A chapter about turning passions into possibilities. We look at ways we can help our girls find and nurture the subjects and hobbies they love.

Building self-esteem in our girls can feel like a long process, but we can speed things along by helping them find the things that make them feel most like themselves. I struggled with seeing the best in myself for a long time and I imagine it's a similar story for many women and girls. We look at our flaws instead of looking at the things that make us feel confident and empowered.

If you have ever heard your daughter say, "I'm not good at anything," then this chapter is for you. Before we dive into the seven conversations in chapter 3, I want to consider how we help our girls find the things they love: their passions, their interests and their hobbies. The things that make them feel most like... themselves. Their true selves. Their best selves.

Helping our girls identify their hobbies and interests is so important because often it will shape the person they become. Although none of us do it on purpose, it is so easy to slip into a negative cycle of thinking about what we can't do rather than what we can. We even do it as adults!

We need to remind our girls how it feels when they're good at something. We see that our girls' confidence grows when they find a topic, subject, sport or activity that they enjoy as well as being good at. We must help our girls define their character and encourage the characteristics that make them who they are. As well as helping them discover their interests, we need to help them grow their strength of heart, for example, by learning how to express gratitude and knowing how to build good relationships. Furthermore, we need to encourage a sense of grit and determination, and support independent thinking, so they're not always following a crowd.

I want to explore what we can do to help our girls find themselves and discover their path to a successful and flourishing future.

What is Success?

Success is often defined by financial achievement, but that really should not be the case. Success, as defined by the dictionary, means "the accomplishment of an aim or purpose". If we support our girls in living their lives with purpose, I believe this could be the key to helping them become a successful and happy individual.

Some might think that you need to be an academic whizz to achieve success, but I'm a good example that that really is not the case. If, like me, you don't feel as though you're academically gifted, it is important to look at smart ways we can live and learn.

So, what makes someone successful? Researchers have been working hard trying to determine what exactly leads a person to be successful. So far, the answer is complicated. While many successful leaders *do* have high salaries and have graduated from elite schools, these aren't necessarily always characteristics of high-achievers. After all, the most successful kid in the neighbourhood may have dropped out of college. Many C-grade students go on to become entrepreneurs, just like me. That's why it is really important to encourage your daughter to work hard at school but, equally, to remind her that grades don't always have to define her career or set her limitations.

That one girl could be a C-grade student just like me who goes on to lead our next wave of young female entrepreneurs. In a world of always thinking bigger, I find it helpful to remember my goal of increasing the self-esteem of one girl at a time; it makes me realise that building on smaller moments can lead to bigger things.

Girls often do great on paper, but when we look at their internal résumé, it doesn't always tell the same story. It is our role as parents, caregivers and teachers to help them find their power and happiness from the inside out. It's about taking it slowly, step-by-step. Only that way can they have boundless opportunities.

We must raise confident girls because they will one day be our leaders. Let us build girls who are not afraid to work hard. Girls who learn how to pick themselves back up when they fall, just like I did. The pressure of grades is huge, but I want to look at things from a different angle. I want to use my own experiences as a positive platform to show all girls, around the world, that they don't always have to conform. To show them that they don't have to be afraid to try something new or take a chance.

When I told my family that I had been offered a publishing contract to write this book, my husband said, "Wow! There you go, kids. Your mum is so smart." However, interestingly enough, despite the compliment, I rarely feel very smart at all. I never ever felt like a smart kid. I was bottom or near the bottom of almost every class. So how do we thrive from the bottom? How do we thrive when we don't feel smart? These are interesting questions that I had to learn how to answer from within myself. I always thought that we stopped learning when we finished school, but how wrong was I? I recently told my daughter that even after school life, you never stop learning. In fact, formal education is just a small part.

So much starts from when we're very young. Whether it's playing with cardboard boxes or making things from milk containers, we can shape our child's creativity from a young age. Free, imaginative play promotes learning and improves memory. Engaging in non-structured play helps kids develop language, spatial intelligence, reasoning and mathematical skills. Could play help children be smarter by the age of seven?

As humans, we are learning all the time, and even if someone isn't top of the class, that doesn't mean they can't naturally develop their intelligence over time or be smart in different ways. In fact, many studies have shown that it is possible to make yourself smarter in various ways, such as reading or playing brain-training games.

Today, our girls have such busy schedules, it can feel like they barely have time to be bored. But, as you would probably suspect, being bored is a good thing. Next time your daughter says she is bored, encourage her to pick up a book. Reading is such a brilliant way to boost her IQ and open her mind to more creative thoughts.

Most kids dread tests, my own daughter especially, but human intelligence and feeling smart should not be measured solely by tests. Surely intelligence should be based around experience? Like allowing children to work through problems and showing them how to find their strengths along the way. Just because I cannot for the life of me resolve one side of a Rubik's Cube (which my son assures me is easy!), that doesn't mean I'm not smart. Quite simply, it's just not the way my brain is wired.

Instead, I worked hard at school, kept my head down in class and, where possible, avoided puzzles and patterns. I enjoy learning new things, and I enjoy the prospect of trying something new along with the challenge of starting a new project. There are many things I have done that have been smart. For example, deciding to write this book was indeed a smart decision. Putting my hand up and choosing to support girls and young women with their confidence and self-esteem – another smart idea. As was starting a parenting blog without fear of failure or judgement.

Over the years, I have learnt that people are smart in different ways. For, despite not having a degree to my name, I somehow find myself publishing my first book. One person's definition of smart might not be the same for someone else.

When we try to help our girls find themselves, and when we look at what makes them unique, perhaps we need to look at things a little bit differently. Many of us are often focused on looking at our children from the outside in. The psychologist Dr Peter Benson, who we will talk about more later on in this chapter, reverses that thought and asks us to look at our children from the inside out. He says that only then will impressive things start to happen.

Have you ever asked your daughter, or a girl you know, to visualise herself as a blank canvas? I hadn't thought of this before, but someone said that you can ask your daughter to draw a simple self-portrait. Then, all around the edges of the picture, ask her to write the things she feels she is "good at" or "capable of".

It is really important to help our girls determine their strengths and then encourage them to put some muscle into it and keep pushing those strengths forward. And I want to show you that many of our girls will thrive from the inside out – which is where they find their strengths.

Dr Howard Gardner, a Professor of Education at Harvard University, states in his book *Frames of Mind: The Theory of Multiple Intelligences* that he believes no individuals should be labelled with just *one specific kind* of intelligence. He believes that people can have multiple strengths, and are, in fact, a unique blend of their strengths. Many of my peers at school were bright and intelligent in different ways, so Dr Gardner's ideas strike true with me.

After spending time working with very different groups – normal and gifted children as well as brain-damaged adults – Dr Gardner developed a way to synthesise his research and observations about how people have many different ways of learning. His theory of multiple intelligences suggests that the traditional notion of intelligence, based on IQ testing, is far too limited. Simply measuring a person's IQ means that we could miss out on other intelligences that an individual may possess. Instead, Dr Gardner proposes eight different intelligences to account for a broader range of human potential in children and adults. These are detailed in the diagram opposite.

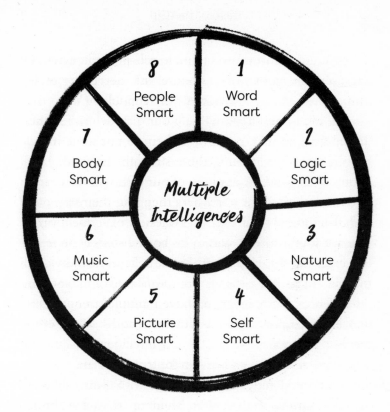

1 Word Smart
  (verbal-linguistic
  intelligence)

2 Logic Smart
  (logical-mathematical
  intelligence)

3 Nature Smart
  (naturalistic intelligence)

4 Self Smart
  (intrapersonal
  intelligence)

5 Picture Smart
  (visual-spatial
  intelligence)

6 Music Smart
  (musical intelligence)

7 Body Smart
  (bodily-kinaesthetic
  intelligence)

8 People Smart
  (interpersonal
  intelligence)

Dr Howard Gardner's eight types of intelligence take into account the fact that different people excel in different areas and learn in different ways.

I love this diagram, and I find so much of it completely relatable. The eight different pockets of intelligence allow us to see what the possibilities are. They allow us to free our minds of what path we or our girls might have thought we wanted to take. The theory expands learning beyond the traditional, school-taught methods and allows us to view success in many different ways.

We know that our schools focus the most attention on verbal-linguistic and logical-mathematical intelligence. I'm not saying this is wrong as, of course, I understand this is an important part of learning. However, we need to give more equal attention to the other types of intelligences: to the artists, architects, musicians, designers, dancers, therapists, entrepreneurs and others who enrich the world in which we live.

I find this theory of multiple intelligences very interesting and very fulfilling, especially for me as a self-aware C-grade student who went on to great things. I'm using different types of intelligence to carve out my own future. For teachers, Gardner's theory is very helpful in understanding the various ways of learning. While one child may prefer a verbal explanation in class, another may prefer "hands-on" learning, and a third may learn better by following pictures or diagrams. This is so important in schools. I personally find this theory useful because two of my children have been identified by their teachers as what we call "visual learners".

Overall, many of us will agree that there is a constant pressure on our children to achieve great grades. But what is the definition of *great*? The pressure in homes around the world increases as homework gets harder, and what we see in real terms is our daughters' frustrations:

wanting to throw her homework book to the floor and shout, "I'm not good at anything!" Sound relatable?

Until recently, researchers believed that the leading factor in a child's success was their cognitive skills – the kind of intelligence that gets measured on IQ tests – including the ability to recognise letters and words. However, today, many say that the most important qualities that lead to success are persistence, self-control, curiosity, grit, conscientiousness, self-confidence and optimism. We will hear about the importance of persistence and optimism from one of our contributors, Nepalese Gurkha and mountaineer Nimsdai Purja, later on in this chapter.

Now, as a parent of a daughter, naturally, I care that she's on the right track academically. I want to know if she's struggling and I want to get her the extra support she needs, if and when she requires it. She has thrown her pencil many times. We breathe. We pick it back up again and we work through it. We persevere.

However, what matters most to me is that she can appreciate the value of hard work. I want her to learn about maths, language and the fascinating world we live in, but test scores and grades are simply benchmarks. I fear they don't tell the whole story. This is why we need to reset what being smart and successful really means.

So, if a girl you know doesn't ace her exams, fear not. We need to remind her that everything will be okay. The key component here is a continued motivation to succeed, whatever their definition of success looks like. This may mean simply finishing the exam or perhaps taking that extra ten minutes to read through their work before handing it in. As a parent, there is one mantra I say to my children often: "Do your best, and dig deep to find the motivation to do that." Ultimately, if a child comes away from an exam, a project or a sports match and they can put their hand on their heart and say, "I did my best," then that should be enough. Doing your best should always be enough, and the way for your child to achieve their best is for them to be able to motivate themselves effectively.

A Question of Motivation

What drives us to do the things we do? What is it that pushes us to accomplish things? Sometimes, the answer may simply be personal gain, but the question is more complex than that. There are many ways to look at the concept of motivation and Dr Howard Gardner has carried out some interesting research on the subject, looking at how we encourage girls to try their best. We need to look at what motivates our girl to embrace her inner strength to succeed.

A key characteristic of "successful" people is their ability to start and complete tasks and projects successfully. So how do they do this? What motivates them?

Dr Gardner explains that motivation can come from the outside (extrinsic motivation) or from the inside (intrinsic motivation). Extrinsic motivation is when someone does something for external rewards or to avoid negative consequences. That means we're not choosing to do the activity because we enjoy it or find it rewarding, but rather because we'll earn something in return or, sometimes, we just have to do it. Intrinsic motivation is when someone does something because they *love to do it* or find it interesting. It means that we perform these tasks for our own sake and are invested in the process, rather than the external reward. The behaviour itself is the reward. Here are some helpful examples:

Extrinsic Motivation

- Keeping your room tidy in exchange for pocket money
- Helping someone for something in return
- Volunteering because it looks good
- Going to new places because you want to tell your friends
- Doing something because you want to look cool

Intrinsic Motivation

- Playing sports because you enjoy how they make you feel
- Using positive affirmations to build a positive mindset
- Saving your pocket money to buy someone a gift
- Reading for enjoyment
- Studying because you want to improve your grades

When we look at these two types of motivation in relation to our education, we see that a willingness to learn for its own sake represents intrinsic motivation, while grades and other accolades represent extrinsic motivation. Research has shown, time and again, that intrinsic motivation leads to more profound learning. The truth is, that the willingness to learn leads to achievement, yet so often achievement is the only part that seems to matter.

My daughter, Erin, will willingly get herself ready for cricket because she enjoys it and finds the sport rewarding in itself. My son Seth feels the same way about football. They don't need any additional promise of reward or fulfilment because just playing the sport does it for them. This is a great example of intrinsic motivation. But when it comes to tidying their bedrooms, they do it because they have to – and to stop the parents from nagging them to do so. This is extrinsic motivation: they don't get any satisfaction from cleaning or tidying.

The psychology of these different motivations is so interesting. It also makes me think of sticker charts – a reward system we've used in our home successfully in the past. But now I'm wondering how successful they really were. When a child reaches ten stickers, they receive a LEGO toy or similar. Sounds good, right? But the problem with bribing children to do something is that they could grow up believing they'll always deserve a reward just for doing what they're expected to do. I don't want my kids asking me what's in it for them every time I need them to do a simple task like brushing their teeth.

Perhaps the easiest way for us to encourage kids to carry out simple tasks is to use mirroring. The more our children see us doing the same action, the more likely they will hopefully *want* to do it for themselves. For example, encourage your daughter brush her own teeth while you brush yours.

Christine Dewart, a US kindergarten teacher, says that when she studied child development at university, she learnt the importance of intrinsic motivation, and there was an emphasis on avoiding too many rewards. But in her everyday professional experience, she sees the value in using rewards to manage her class – and has found that "acknowledging one student's good behaviour helps other students do the same."

I have considered whether it would be possible to boost intrinsic motivation. Or if we can make the switch from being extrinsically to intrinsically motivated. Our girls can start to boost their intrinsic motivation by thinking about goals that are important to them and writing them down. Finding the things they are passionate about will motivate them to find ways to do them more. Overall, let us not forget, our girls are growing, developing and building up an array of experiences that, as they learn which things they love to do, will provide the basis for intrinsic motivation. So if they need a little extrinsic motivation to master a new skill or to encourage them to step into unfamiliar territory, then I think that's okay. The key is finding the right balance of both.

Finding Their Spark

As tweens and teens struggle with anxiety, how can we help them discover who they are and what makes them tick? With so many external influences, such as peer pressure, our girls can struggle to identify with their own sense of self. They can get so caught in a bubble of comparing themselves to others (so easily done), it can be difficult for them to remember what makes them unique. When mixing the real world and the online world, things can become blurred.

Supporting girls in recognising their talents and interests is a brilliant way to help them cultivate their strengths. Your daughter may think she didn't do well in that science project, but she lights up when she's outside on the athletics track. Then there's that quiet girl who sits at the back of the class. Who knew she wrote amazing stories and poetry?

Having aspirations is important at any age, but when it comes to finding our girls' passions, we should start small but think big. Crucially, it is never too late to get started. From a young age, the professions to which they aspire are often the ones they see in their immediate environment, so showing them other ideas will broaden their sphere. Similarly, if they could be influenced by negatives in their environment, help them see life beyond this by explicitly sharing your belief in them and showing them different examples.

We need to turn our attention inwards to find our passions, to embrace our strengths and the qualities that make us unique. It's about raising girls to be kind, compassionate, helpful and confident. The qualities I really would like my daughter to cultivate include friendship, teamwork and generosity. I regularly remind Erin that when things get hard – and they most certainly will – almost everything can become just a little easier to handle with a few good, deep breaths. I tell her that, although I hope she gets decent grades and works hard at school, what I really care about is the person she is *becoming*. So how do I help her *become*?

Firstly, it's about me taking the time to understand her passions, her sparks, the things that make her tick. As parents, we must encourage our children to identify and develop these sparks. Many girls will find their own passions along the way, but don't be afraid to support them in seeking out their sparks. Supporting our girls in finding themselves and understanding their own self-worth is no easy task, but when we highlight and encourage their interests and skills, our girls start to feel more self-confident, capable and inspired.

Secondly, it's important to remember that your daughter's passions won't necessarily be the same as yours or her friends. Just because a friend has started a new hobby or found something they love, she shouldn't feel pressured to fall in love with it too. What's important here, and what I want you to take from this chapter, is that the need to communicate that giving things a *try* is what is important. Over the years, my daughter has tried many things: new topics, hobbies, clubs and sports. She most definitely does not love them all and many don't fuel her spark. However, there are a few – just a handful of these – that light her up. That make her… well… *her*.

For my first contributor in this chapter, I wanted to find someone who truly discovered their passion by accident. Someone who tried something new without being afraid and never looked back. In fact, her decision to give something a try ended up shaping her life.

Rochelle "Rocky" Clark MBE is the most capped England rugby player (as of June 2021), a true ambassador for girls and young women all over the world. Since making her rugby debut in 2003, Clark has gone on to win seven Six Nations titles and was part of the Red Roses squad when they won the coveted Women's Rugby World Cup trophy in 2014. Rocky was honoured with an MBE for services to rugby in 2015, and she retired from international rugby in 2018.

You Win Just by Giving it a Go
by Rochelle "Rocky" Clark MBE

I have always been a little bit of a show-off. I was quite a chunky kid, certainly between the ages of twelve and twenty. I lacked confidence around those I didn't know, and I was a bit nervous about putting myself out there.

I have always been sporty, but I'd always been a big girl. I loved it and I'd get thrown into the goalkeeper and goal defence positions. I enjoyed being part of a team, but I hadn't found a passion in anything, until I found rugby. I was at school, and a friend was playing rugby – I thought it was definitely not my sport. When the team was low on numbers, I stepped into a training session and had no idea what was going on. I didn't know which way to run or where the ball should be passed, but somehow, I ended up playing in the game the next week. I remember asking the coach, "Isn't there meant to be something about tackling?" to which he replied, "Run, grab my legs, and lasso me to the floor." And that was how I learnt to play rugby. Rugby led me to make friends, and I realised I was actually quite good at something, that there was something I could bring to the team.

It was only when I started rugby that I realised I was a big asset to the team because of my size. They wanted big girls that could run as I could. People were grateful to have me on their team, and that gave me a huge amount of confidence. Pushing myself out of my comfort zone used to be hard, but once I found that confidence, I never looked back.

I joined my local adult team, which you can join at age sixteen, and I played a couple of friendly games. The

70

coaches said they were impressed with my natural skills and ability. Over time, the coaches shaped me and worked hard to improve my skills further. I was sixteen but playing alongside others in their late thirties – and I was running rings round them. Our team kept getting promoted and eventually played premiership. My big opportunity came when I was training with South England Students. At a player development academy, I was picked to play in an England Under 19's game. From there, I was spotted and put into Emerging England, then England Academy.

I really wanted to go on an England Academy team tour to South Africa, and I remember getting the call, "Sorry Rocky, you aren't going on the South Africa tour. In fact, you're coming on the England senior tour to Canada!" I didn't know what to say – I had just jumped a level! They got me capped and got me fit for the next year, and I ended up playing for the seniors for the best part of fifteen years!

I found myself feeling invincible – and I found my confidence. I still get this today. I often think back to that first training session, and I realise that if I'd never taken that opportunity, and never stepped out of my comfort zone, I would never have had all the amazing experiences I have. In rugby, you're pushed to a place that's really hard. But you get through it – and that's the best feeling.

Losing is a huge part of developing as an individual – in your personal life and your sporting life. You need to be okay with it. The biggest thing I have learnt is to grow and learn from any loss and any perceived failure. You have learnt what not to do, and how that feels. Now is the opportunity to try something different and learn *from ourselves. When you're younger, the importance of winning and losing isn't there – I was there to have fun and enjoy my sport. And as long as I had done my best, I was happy.*

I've now played in four world cup finals and we won one. Having lost, I walked away knowing that I had done all that I could do, and that's that. We would train more for the next chance. Sometimes losses are sent to test you, but the biggest thing is how you get over them and keep moving forward. Don't be afraid to be down, sad and upset about losing and failing – but use that motivation to pick yourself up and go again.

The 2014 Rugby World Cup was a really tight game. It was hard and fast. Canada were a fit team, and as we neared the end of the game, despite us being ahead, our team were panicking, running and trying to keep up. When the final whistle went, I remember dropping to my knees, overwhelmed, and I thought, "Wow, we've done it!" Eyes wide, smiling, screaming, we all just thought, "We've actually done it!" Eight years on from my first world cup – when I felt what dreams were made of – it still brings back such great memories. It was a surreal feeling. I remember just trotting around after, wearing my medal – I couldn't take it off!

We want to raise self-confident girls, today and tomorrow. We know that teenage girls struggle sometimes with how they feel and knowing what to do. My advice would be to give girls the opportunity to try new things. It might be that they have never found that thing that brings them joy, whether that's a team sport or a dance class. Just being active is a huge celebration for girls, and it helps to build their confidence. It's important for them

"Don't be afraid to be down, sad and upset about losing and failing – but use that motivation to pick yourself up and go again."

ROCHELLE "ROCKY" CLARK MBE

to take the first step in getting out there and trying new things. We also need to recognise their achievements. It's not about winning and losing. We need to reward our girls for their effort and their ability to show sportsmanship.

You've got to try things and make your own decisions. You're going to like some things, and you aren't going to like others, but you need to put yourself out there to try – else you'll never know. You lose nothing by giving something a go."

———

There are so many things I take from Rocky's story and, more than anything, it's her constant courage and resilience. Courage is just one of the amazing qualities that we learn from professional athletes. Rocky's career started with a willingness to try something different – proof that we never find success without first having the courage to try.

So much more is learnt through the power of sport than you might think. As parents and caregivers, we recognise that there is a lot more to a game than simply winning. Participating in matches and competitions teaches our girls about the importance of teamwork, commitment to a task, cooperation and how to respect the opponent. Every game is also an opportunity for children to learn, and every game should be entered into with a winning mindset.

It is hard to imagine someone like Rocky, a world cup winner and an MBE, talking about losing. For our girls, losing shouldn't be avoided – it shows them they need to work hard in order to have success, because good things aren't just handed to them. We find personal growth through losing games. Rocky will simply train harder to come back stronger, match after match. It is courage, resilience and a winning spirit that we see in all professional athletes, just like Rocky. Performing your best, no matter what level of sport or activity you partake in, requires mental strength. Whatever your daughter might be facing right now, Rocky gives us an important reminder that disappointment doesn't mean that you failed; it means that you tried.

Turning Passions into Possibilities

Dr Peter Benson is a scientist and researcher. He is renowned as one of the world's leading experts on adolescence. His central idea is that everyone has a spark, and that these sparks can ignite a vocation or career, which will lead to an enriched, thriving life. Dr Benson explains that children and young teenagers aged 10–14 almost always have something inside them, whether it be an interest, enthusiasm, talent or passion. That spark could be the making of them in later life. He said, "The idea of spark is very much like the idea of spirit. The word spirit comes from Latin and means 'my breath, put into the world with vigour and courage'." I love this idea. The idea of lighting up our daughters from the inside out. But, in terms of finding their spark, how on earth do we do that? Where do we start?

Most of us, in my opinion, will find our passions – our sparks – between the ages of 10–20. As you discover your passion, you'll start to thrive on the inside. You'll feel that affirmation; you'll find the courage to go forward with your aspirations. What it is you are feeling – will feel right.

In chapter 1, we learnt how a child's identity begins forming from the moment they are born. Between the ages of three to five, children may talk of wanting to be animals or fantastical creatures (such as unipugs). But by the age of seven, these ambitions turn into more viable occupational aspirations, influenced by the people they meet and their immediate environment. Whatever our children's ambitions may be, we, as parents, need to actively encourage and nurture their passions.

I've often spoken to students about turning passions into possibilities. It's a phrase that brings me so much joy when I say it out loud. Once we find things we're passionate about, we realise how much joy and happiness that can bring. A friend recently asked me a question on this topic: "What's more important – should girls do the things they're good at, or the things they love? Is it even possible to combine the two?"

I am still considering my answer. Of course, if you can do the things you love as your career, then you have hit the jackpot, but for many, that's not the reality. But talent and passion can be two sides of the same coin. The starting ingredients are talent, interest and enjoyment. They lead to skill, knowledge and experience. Passion is always a great starting point for side-projects and hobbies, and, for our girls, we need to support them in finding interests which spark their personal joy.

So, what type of spark does your daughter have?

Is it a skill or a talent? For instance, is she a good dancer, writer, artist, athlete, creator or musician?

Or is her spark a commitment? She may be someone who is passionate about protecting the natural world, the environment or how people are treated. It could be that she's a generous, caring person who wants to channel her positivity for the benefit of others.

Perhaps she has strong, defined characteristics. Think about her main qualities. Is she a communicator – sociable, empathetic, confident? Could she be that "go to" person – the one who speaks up and takes the lead? Is she a problem -solver, a person of trust, a person that others rely on?

Dr Benson's research identified more than 220 types of sparks. Here are just some of his definitions of what a spark can do:

- Give energy and joy
- Provide the feeling of being alive, useful and purposeful
- Be so absorbing to the point that you "lose yourself in the moment"
- Originate from inside a person
- Be a skill, talent, interest or gift
- Be a person's prime source of meaning, self-directed action and purpose
- Have the potential to make the world a better place for others

Looking at this list, can your daughter identify which type of spark she has?

Why not discuss these definitions with your family and take the time to listen to what type of sparks your children think they're best matched to.

The important element now, once your daughter has identified her spark, is to focus on how she can use it and apply it. Ask other family members to support her. Be aware that her spark may change, and that's okay – it's part of growing up. But her sparks, whatever they are, will always be the heart of who she is.

What I find most significant from the insights of Dr Benson is that he really wanted to shift the way educators think about young people. Instead of educators focusing on what's wrong with children and trying to fix them, he flipped this on its head and asked educators to focus on what was right with kids – and to support them.

Looking Beyond the Possible

I am so fortunate that I have met and spoken to so many incredible individuals during the writing of this book. Sometimes you have the opportunity to talk to people who have achieved things that many have not. I wonder what we can learn from individuals who believe in making the impossible possible. It takes a certain kind of mindset and strength of character to push yourself (body and mind) to the outer limits. To the point that when you think all hope is lost, you find a way. That kind of strength lies within Nimsdai Purja.

In 2021, Nirmal "Nimsdai" Purja MBE became the fastest person ever to climb all fourteen of the world's highest mountains. The previous world record for this achievement was just under eight years... Nimsdai smashed this project in six months and six days. The peaks – all within the Himalayan and Karakoram mountain ranges – were not selected because of their infamous technical challenges, but rather for the one thing they have in common: they're the only summits on Earth higher than 8,000 metres, and they're all located in the notorious "death zone" where human life cannot exist.

Only forty climbers have achieved the feat of ascending all fourteen of these peaks. Nimsdai's vision was to rewrite the history books in a monumental manner, which naturally attracted many sceptics. To many, Nimsdai's project seemed impossible, despite his expedition title, Project Possible.

I wonder if some people feel a greater sense of purpose, and whether that's what provides the motivation for them to keep on going, even through difficult times. For someone like Nimsdai, when they find themselves wanting to slow down or take a break, they remind themselves of what they are trying to do, and they suddenly feel the urge to continue.

Nimsdai kindly spoke to me about making the impossible possible. I wondered what kind of mindset is needed to make that happen? It must be more than just setting your mind to something. It must be about *truly* setting your sights on a purpose that can't be disrupted no matter how much noisy negativity it attracts. Whatever happens, you'll try, and, where necessary, you'll try again. There's a burning desire to achieve your goal. That's what great people do. From world-class entrepreneurs to Olympic athletes – they achieve incredible things. In Nimsdai's case, they break records doing it.

Nimsdai believes you can do anything you set your mind to, but it takes courage, belief, truth in yourself, perseverance and an ability to face your fears. I suppose in many ways, for all of us, when it comes to ambition, *setting* goals is easy. Following them through is the hardest part.

I asked Nimsdai where he got his passion for climbing from. He says that he never set out to become a climber. Born in the Dhaulagiri region of Nepal, Nimsdai was raised in Chitwan, in the country's flatlands. His first passion in life was to be a Gurkha – a soldier that serves in a unique Nepalese unit of the British Army.

In 2003, he achieved that goal and left home for the Gurkhas, where he served for six years before passing Special Forces selection and joining the SBS (Special Boat Service). He went on to have a distinguished military career. He gently taps his chest a number of times as he talks so intensely about what it means to him to serve Queen and Country. It makes me feel very proud to be British. Now Nimsdai stands as one of the mountaineering greats and will continue to push the boundaries of what is humanly possible.

———

Never Give Up
by Nirmal "Nimsdai" Purja MBE

My mother is a lady who never gave up. She gave me her today – for my future. She wouldn't eat the food she desired because she would rather sacrifice it for her kids. "Mum" is a very powerful word. Every mum out there in the world will always love their children. There is a saying in Nepalese: "Other than your children, everything you see could be better. We are always looking at things as if they're not the best – other than our children."

I know my mum is so proud of me. She passed away shortly after Project Possible, but she set me up in life to achieve what I have. Even from a young age, I started exploring. I would often go into the jungle by myself. When I was a kid, my ambition was to be a Gurkha. It was normal for me to go off at 1am and run twenty to thirty kilometres. I gave 100 per cent to everything and, for me, it was natural to go from Gurkha to Special Forces. I became the first Gurkha to pass the selection for the SBS (Special Boat Service).

If anybody wants to achieve something, they need two things: passion and to work hard. I work hard for what I achieve – and that is how you achieve. I will always tell kids (both boys and girls) that other than passion and hard work, the other most important thing in life is self-confidence. If you don't trust yourself, and don't believe yourself, then who is going to believe in you? No one can take away my self-belief, and that is how I got somewhere. At the end of the day, you are you. We all have our own mountains to climb, but we must believe in ourselves to get there and overcome those challenges. The key is to never give up. It will always be tough to reach a summit but nothing good in life comes easy.

My mindset has always been positive. I am always competing against myself, never anyone else. I'm all about running faster than I did before, getting better at being me. There are two ways to look at this. If I'm running against Usain Bolt, I'm not going to beat him because he's Bolt. However, we all have our own strengths. Our strengths and weaknesses must be bespoke to ourselves; we cannot be everybody else. It's about your personal best, not anybody else's. Personal satisfaction is the biggest asset we can have in life.

I strive to achieve my "Personal Pursuit of Excellence" by giving 100 per cent in everything I do. If you do your best, then there are no regrets. If you have tried your best and feel like you could not give any more, you will sleep

"Challenges should excite us because we only get stronger as we overcome these problems."

NIRMAL "NIMSDAI" PURJA MBE

well at night. That's what it comes down to. For me, I love climbing. Climbing is my thing, and it's who I want to be. But it takes hard work, dedication and effort to get there.

Until I was almost thirty years old, climbing Everest never even crossed my mind. I went to see Everest one day and that's when I decided to climb. It is never too late to start something new. We only have one life and so, whatever time in that life inspiration hits you, own it. Things in life don't always go to plan, but that's the beauty of it. Challenges should excite us because we only get stronger as we overcome these problems. The challenges we overcome build who we are. On that note, I always have a plan B, a plan C and so on – but I never focus on that plan B because focusing on plan B and thinking about failure will ultimately lead to failure.

I climbed the world's fourteen highest peaks in the fastest time – just six months and six days. When I first suggested Project Possible, no one believed it could happen. It was beyond people's imagination, so I had very little support. Nevertheless, I put everything on the line and believed in myself. I never let my asthma hold back my potential. Everything is a mind game, and my mental strength was so strong that I felt I could overcome that hurdle. I acclimatised and adapted. Project Possible became possible because I just went for it. I gave my all until I got the result I wanted. Here are some of my thoughts on how you too can achieve your best:

Your mental strength is so important. Learn how to perform under pressure, as that's how you can develop the strength you never knew you had.

Strive to your own strengths and weaknesses, not anybody else's.

In order to achieve, you need both passion and hard work.
If you don't believe in yourself, how is anybody else going to believe in you?
Failure is not an option.
Always have a back-up plan.
Never give up.

———

What I have learnt most from Nimsdai's words is that the best way to spark passion in your girls is to help them do the things that make them feel good. Whether it's trying new things in the hope it will ignite a passion, or developing hobbies and interests that they already enjoy, finding that spark can really help ignite passion and creativity in other areas of your girl's life. Hobbies and interests can be found anywhere and everywhere. If an opportunity presents itself, encourage your girl to try it out. Maybe it's taking a dance class, trying a new sport, joining Brownies or even doing some volunteer work. Overall, we must help our girls do the things they feel good about choosing to do.

Going back to Dr Benson's idea that a single spark could change a young person's life, we need to realise that everyone truly does have a "spark" – and by plugging into what that spark is, it could honestly be the most important part of your daughter's journey on her way to finding herself.

Seven Ways to Help Your Daughter Find Her Spark

1. **Try lots of different things**
   I really can't stress the importance of this one enough. Encourage your girl to have plenty of interests. When she's on the journey to figuring out what she loves most, this is one of the most crucial steps and it's actually quite simple:

   Do things.

   Do a lot of things.

   It's better to have lots of options and interests than none at all.

2. **Make a list of all the things she is interested in**
   Once she has created her list, ask her to pick two things to focus on first. Try to find ways to advance those two passions and see if these things are something she really wants to pursue further. If she realises it's not what she thought it would be, mark it off of the list and edit the list together to look for other opportunities.

3. **Remind her to always stay true to herself**
   Your daughter is entitled to change her mind whenever she wants, but if she wants to stop something, ask her why. Help her take the next steps towards finding that thing that encourages her to be herself.

4. **She doesn't have to feel defined by one thing**

As much as I love writing, I'm also passionate about being a woman in tech. I do many different things and I juggle them all. I'm not doing everything perfectly, but I enjoy them all. Your daughter most definitely doesn't have to be defined by one thing.

5. **She should focus on herself**

However she goes about finding her passion, she definitely won't find it by watching and comparing herself to others. It doesn't matter if her friends are further along in their school life or early career than she is, and if someone looks like they have everything figured out, in most cases, they probably don't. Remind your daughter not to compare her journey to others. It's important that she focuses on *her* journey, wherever it leads.

6. **Let go of fear**

Many of us decide not to try new things because of the fear that it will go wrong or that we will make a mistake. However, if we always think like this we could pass up an amazing opportunity – all because we couldn't find the strength to take the first step. I don't know about you, but I don't like walking around in the dark. Remind your daughter that sometimes you have to feel the fear, you have to fumble in the dark, but you should do it anyway. Taking opportunity and managing uncertainty are all part of the journey. In order to help her find her passion, big leaps of faith are mandatory.

7. **Find stillness**

Finding stillness is not as easy as it seems. Girls rarely stand still. They have so many thoughts, ideas and emotions swarming through their minds that they get frustrated when they can't seem to figure things out. Sometimes simply reminding our girls to take a moment of stillness, to simply do nothing, is just what they need. However our girls find their passions, there is no rush. At some point, your daughter will find the passions that light her up. As the Greek philosopher Plutarch once said, "Youth are not vessels to be filled, but fires to be lit."

Chapter 3

EMPOWERING CONVERSATIONS

In this chapter, I want to support you in dealing with tricky questions or statements you may get from your daughter. I think that if we put extra effort into our conversations with our daughters, it could help us interact more positively in those moments. Each empowering conversation in this chapter has a different topic and is accompanied by support, tips and words of wisdom from some wonderful contributors. There are many other conversations that I'm sure will come up between you and your daughter, but I hope that the advice in this chapter will help increase your creativity as to how you approach any future conversations. So next time you get in a pickle with an awkward question, think back to some of the suggestions here and use the ideas in your conversation. You'll be surprised by just how much these stories and tips can impact your daughter in a really positive way.

Conversation 1: "I don't like putting my hand up in class!"

How do we teach our girls to take risks, even if the risks are small?

Sometimes as adults we don't put our hand in the air for fear of saying something incorrect or something that might sound silly. Then, it always happens. Someone next to you shoots up their hand and says the exact same thing *you* were thinking! This even happens to me now… and I'm a middle-aged woman! You always wish you had put your hand up in the first place, and it is at that moment you promise yourself you'll put your hand up next time. I repeat, next time.

So, if as adults we still have these apprehensions about raising our hands, perhaps we have glossed over how not putting our hands up affects us throughout our life. More importantly, what do we say to our girls who are equally afraid of raising their hands? We have an overwhelming fear that we will say something, and the entire room will burst out laughing. But quite honestly, how often does that happen – and is it not better to be inquisitive than never to ask?

If a girl in a class is 75 per cent sure of the answer to a question but not 100 per cent, I would still encourage her to raise her hand in class. I would argue that education isn't always about getting the answers right every time, but it's more about encouraging productive thinking, which can last a lifetime. Let us start by asking our girls what they put their hand up for today, or if, when she did raise her hand, the teacher called on her?

Be a Good Girl

Research from *Science* magazine shows that girls, at the age of six, believe they are less likely than boys to be "really, really smart". This isn't the news I want to hear.

From a young age, many girls are told to "be a good girl" – and, I will be honest, I said this so many times to my own daughter when she was younger. It hadn't even crossed my mind that this direct phrase could be a potential issue. According to the study, self-doubt creeps in and, slowly, girls start worrying about stepping out of line and making mistakes.

Praising girls for being "good" is common. But what is "good"? There's the generalisation that girls need to play nicely and be quiet to be considered good. Whereas for boys, we expect them to get messy, play fight and be loud with their voices. But girls are diverse, and they like different things. Some like trucks and tractors whilst some like dolls and dancing. Girls can be outspoken, spirited, messy – and they can be shy and quiet too. Often, parents will praise their girls for sitting or playing quietly by saying "good girl", reinforcing the stereotype that a good girl is a quiet girl. Perhaps we should stop praising girls for being "good" and instead focus on praising them for their actions instead.

In a long-term study published in *Child Development* journal, a diverse group of more than fifty toddlers were videotaped as they interacted with their parents. This was done at the ages of one, two and three. Parents who said "good job" were considered by the researchers to be praising the child's actions, whereas the parents who said "good girl" were considered to be praising the individual. To you and me, that may seem like such a small and subtle difference, but apparently toddlers can feel the difference. Five years later, the children who were praised more for what they did than for who they were ended up being better equipped to take on challenges: they were able to come up with more strategies for dealing with setbacks, and they indicated that they welcomed challenges over simple tasks.

The researchers didn't find that praising the individual stunted the children in any way (thank goodness!), but the study really made me wonder about how we praise our children and how important it is to think about what we choose to praise and how we do it. For example, girls are often praised for being quiet rather than for using their voice. It's an interesting way of looking at things, isn't it?

When I was out walking with a friend recently, she asked me where my passion for discussing confidence came from. It took me a moment to consider my reply. I told her about how, although I was a confident kid, I never really allowed my own voice or my opinions to come out. I was always considered a "good girl". I rarely stepped out of line during my school years, and my mum recently reminded me that I was a quiet but content child. Looking back, I see now how I was guided by other people's opinions, but I hardly stopped to take a breath and think about using my own voice. I was so set on agreeing with others or following in the footsteps of others, particularly my older brother. He was probably an early role model for me, which he hadn't signed up for. My entire childhood was about following him around to see what he did. As he was the eldest, whatever he did, I did. I will never be the eldest so I will never know, but I imagine for anyone reading this, if you are the firstborn, it must have come with a level of responsibility. Can it sometimes feel like a burden? As a middle child, I often wonder.

So, what can we do to avoid the "good girl" mentality – or good girl syndrome? The general consensus seems to be that if we want to comment or praise, we should focus on the action and the effort, rather than labelling our children as being good or bad. Although there isn't always a right or wrong approach to this, perhaps we can focus on phrases such as, "thank you for putting your shoes away when I asked, that was very helpful," as opposed to, "thank you for being a good girl."

After further research, I came across a study on gender bias in education, which asserts that girls, from a very young age, are socialised to view assertiveness as an essentially masculine quality. The study goes on to say that assertive behaviour from girls can often be regarded as disruptive and can be viewed in a negative way by adults. Therefore, the pressure to speak up, to voice their opinions, is tied in with how it will make them look. Girls are conditioned, in a way, to be pleasing, quiet and nice. It goes without saying that this is not typical of all female students, but I do find it interesting how assertiveness can be valued as a negative quality rather than a positive one.

This seems like the perfect time to introduce our next contributor: a woman who has been working hard to ensure her voice is heard. Anna Whitehouse, better known as Mother Pukka, is a British journalist, author, TEDx speaker, radio presenter and activist. In recent years, Anna spoke at the famous London landmark, Trafalgar Square, to raise awareness of the need for

"The biggest issue
for young girls is
having confidence
in their own voice."

ANNA WHITEHOUSE

improvements to flexible working hours, following her #FlexAppeal campaign.

The Flex Appeal campaign started after Anna was late to pick up her child from nursery after a fellow commuter got her bag stuck in the train doors. Anna was reprimanded. She asked her employer for more flexible working hours, but her request was rejected – and so Anna quit. Anna used her voice to launch #FlexAppeal and rolled out events across the UK to encourage people to ask for flexible working in their workplace. Evidence from her campaign has since been used by the Welsh Assembly to suggest that universal flexible working could help close the gender pay gap.

———

Finding Your Voice
by Anna Whitehouse

Girls don't put their hands up if they don't feel 100 per cent confident in their answer. I find that the biggest issue for young girls is having confidence in their own voice, which is going to be very different from other people's voices.

It was quietly suggested to me when I was younger that I shouldn't do A-level English because I would always see the colour in literature, which wasn't really the substantial scene – my mind would analyse literature in a way that was different to other people. But what I took from that, was that I wasn't substantial enough.

It can take only a very small comment from anyone – a comment that could even be well meaning – to shatter confidence in a young woman, who is trying to build her confidence and find out who she is.

I think the biggest turning point for me was realising that I don't need to know the answer to ask the questions. The failure I have had is what has built my success. My past has involved standing in front of a crowd, quite clearly making a mistake – and feeling it – and turning that into success for my future. I think it's our complete fear of failure, or wondering what others think, that shatters that confidence in women. A lot of women tend to have a very high emotional intelligence in that sense.

Even in adult women, we downplay our salaries by 8 per cent, whereas men up-play their salaries by 6 per cent. We are embarrassed by doing well. So, for women, it looks like success and getting the answer right are both issues. If we're constantly held down by the fear of failure, or even fear of success, we're not going to move forward.

Statistics show that men don't tend to have the same issue. They fail, and they move on. They go on to succeed, and they get celebrated for succeeding. Women need to celebrate their successes. We need to celebrate success and overcome that fear of failure.

My first business was a dog-walking business called Doggy Style. I was charging £20 an hour, which was an extortionate rate back in the day. I called it Doggy Style because it fit my personality, though others always said to me, "Pipe down, you won't be taken seriously." There might be elements of your personality that don't sit well with what people have known before. But that's why you have to keep pushing yourself out there, because doing that will open the door for other people with those same personality traits. You have to be yourself – and bring yourself to your ABCs, your GCSEs, your A-levels, your university career and your first job. You have to bring yourself. We, as women, have been silencing ourselves and dumbing ourselves down for so long in this patriarchal system. Now is the time to be yourself, failure and all.

If, at ten years old, your daughter isn't putting her hand up for fear of giving an "imperfect" answer, what's going to happen twenty years down the line, when she's afraid to raise her hand for that promotion?

When thinking of my own daughters, I want them to learn that they don't need to "man up" in order to be heard and have a place at the table. The advice I have for them is the advice that I have given to many women, and to myself: "You don't need to be loud, or something you're not, to be heard." Celebrate and show your femininity in the workplace. Don't man up. You can be soft in business and still successful – because soft does not mean weak. Too often women feel that they struggle to be heard, and struggle to get their point across.

If you have someone bulldozing away with a point, I find the best way to be heard is to put a placeholder in that conversation. Whether it's at school or in a boardroom meeting, gently interrupt and then let them continue – just by interjecting, people will know to come to you next. Using that soft, gentle placeholder will show people that you want to be heard and it will present you as firm in the end. Present yourself in the way you want to present yourself. You don't need to shout louder to be heard. Don't see softness as weakness.

And another thing: Stop dumbing down the messages. Stop treating children like children and talk to them about the failures you have faced and overcome. Tell children stories of your life – of your absolute peak and your crushing lowest. You can be very honest with children, who have been babyfied in many ways and deemed not ready for these messages. We should build children up to recognise that there will be a fall at some point, but show them how Mummy got back up and dusted herself off and moved forward. If all they see is Mummy's success story, her business and so on, they will see themselves as failures. Show them who you truly are.

I told my daughter of my miscarriage when she was just four years old, because she asked. And from there we had a conversation that resulted in my young daughter supporting me through a tough time. If we aren't honest with our children, how can we prepare them for life? And you've got to do that in your own way. Don't follow my lead, or someone else's lead; you know your children, but don't be afraid of showing them the light and the dark.

Just as importantly, we must give our children freedom. My daughter currently wants to be a seagull catcher. She had her chicken nugget stolen by a seagull once and now she feels there's a gap in the market for seagull catching. And you know what, I told her to go for it. I think we are the first generation not to shoehorn our hopes and dreams onto our children. I feel the shift now. In the past it was natural to drive our children towards a vocational career – a doctor, a nurse, an accountant. Yes, they're exceptional roles, but they are not everyone's roles.

And they are not the only roles I want my daughters to feel they must fit into. I think that by building up the world your young children want to go into will build upon their confidence. My daughter says she wants to be a mummy, and I tell her that's a huge job! I tell them every night, "You can do anything."

At college, I didn't have my voice. I felt that my voice wasn't the right voice – that it didn't fit in, so it was better to be quiet. Once I realised that, yes, there will be people who don't think you should be speaking, but you speak regardless, my confidence grew. Blocking out the white noise of other people's own issues and own insecurities is the big challenge. You need to block that out to build your own confidence. If you're waiting for perfection, you're going to miss your chance. Receiving negative comments can be difficult, but repackage that as someone else's experience jarring with yours, and open a conversation around their perspective; don't fault your own.

Step back from trying to operate perfectly, waiting for the right time and being someone. You are now. Step back from worrying about backlash. That will be the moment you are heard. Where do you want to be heard? Invest in your family, your friends; invest in your home. Listen to yourself and block out the white noise of others telling you what you should be.

———

Anna's words are a brilliant reminder about the importance of finding our voice. By finding hers, she built a platform that led to her flexible working campaign being heard in Parliament. In July 2019, a bill was introduced requiring employers to offer flexible working in employment contracts and to advertise vacancies as suitable for flexible working unless certain conditions are met. Anna demonstrates that you don't have to be an outspoken, loud person to lead. She has proved that it comes down to respect. If others respect what you have to say, they will listen. You don't have to be loud to be heard.

Finding their Power

Women and girls can be powerful, and no one can deny that more girl power is needed in this world. We're not talking pink doll's houses and fluffy kittens here. We are talking about helping our girls find their voice. Ultimately, we need more female role models, we need more female leaders – and we can find future leaders in almost every classroom. We need to find those girls who are putting their hands up from a young age, and find those who are not.

So where do we start?

We should talk to girls about leadership and allow them to lead when they're young. Leadership skills build confidence, and they become second nature to girls if we create opportunities for them to make decisions and solve problems. We need girls to be able to listen to their own feelings, to follow their gut, to recognise their right to say no and to know the right times to say yes! Let's teach our girls that what they feel and want is valid, and that they do have a voice.

Facebook's chief operating officer, Sheryl Sandberg, once said that one of the biggest obstacles to the women of today achieving success is a lack of confidence and bravery in voicing our thoughts and ideas. Specifically, she said, "We need to teach women to raise their hands more."

I considered what impact it could have if we taught our girls how to use their voice and how to feel more confident raising their hand. When girls learn to use their

Ultimately, we need more female role models, we need more female leaders – and we can find future leaders in almost every classroom.

own assertive voice, they are likely to perform better at school. Those who learn how to communicate well at school are more likely to be able to stand up to negative peer pressure and have a better way of verbalising their feelings to friends and family.

There are many ways you can start encouraging your daughter to raise her hand. Tell her that, for one thing, she will start to feel more self-assured every time she speaks up. And another good reason? Her teacher will appreciate her participation. It shows the teacher that she cares about her classroom performance. Let's keep on raising our hands and, when we're called on, help our girls to raise the confidence bar at the same time.

My daughter used to be a brilliant example of this. She never willingly raised her hand in class and she openly told me this. She was so fearful of getting the wrong answer. However, in more recent times, I witnessed something magical. From afar, I was watching her have a sports lesson. I had parked up at a coffee shop around the back of the pitch. I could see her, but she didn't see me. A line of around twelve girls stood in front of a teacher they had never met before. I could see that the teacher was speaking and making hand gestures, although I was too far away to hear what was being said. She was asking the girls a question. No one raised their hand. Then suddenly, out of the blue, I watched my daughter, Erin, shoot her hand up in the air! She was the only one to do so. Then the teacher asked another question and again, Erin shot up her hand. I was blown away by what I was witnessing.

My daughter, confidently raising her hand. I won't forget what I saw that day. I saw hope. I saw that change is coming. Even if it is one girl at a time.

When we consider the importance of raising one's hand, I wondered how a father of five daughters would approach this subject. Raising one daughter is a busy job in itself, so how would it feel to raise five? I invited Lorenzo Colangelo, British entrepreneur and owner of The Gallery hair and beauty salon, to be a contributor to my book. Lorenzo, in my view, is someone who has always had high ambitions. He has turned his salon into an award-winning organisation, achieving the hairdressing business award, "Salon of The Year", for three successive years. I wondered if his entrepreneurial flair runs in the blood of his daughters as well and what experiences he can share from raising five girls.

Fathers can have such a positive, far-reaching influence on their daughters' lives, and I wanted to explore how Lorenzo supported and guided his five daughters through the challenges of their teenage years and beyond. Fathers and daughters who participate in activities together, especially athletic activities or working together, can help make the bond closer. As an entrepreneur, Lorenzo is a natural risk-taker and will be used to putting his hand up to take an opportunity. Since supporting our girls to raise their hands from a young age is crucial, I wondered how Lorenzo taught his daughters to do just that.

———

Every Girl is Different
by Lorenzo Colangelo

I have five daughters, ranging from twenty to twenty-eight years old.

When I was at the tender age of twenty-two, my eldest was born. It was all a bit scary to be honest. Jasmin arrived two weeks early, after a pretty uncomfortable drive up to Manchester for a trip to see Les Misérables. *At 5am, my wife thought she had wet the bed, and Jasmin was born 1:30pm that same day. As a young dad, I did not feel fully equipped. I had never studied parenting and had never really considered having children. Although we had had nine months to prepare, I don't think anything can ever prepare you for that moment you first hold your baby. I just remember making lots of promises to my daughter. I wanted to be the best I could be for her.*

Jasmin was barely two years old when we had our twins, Sienna and Blaise. Our family of three adapted to becoming a family of five. My wife is amazing. As a father, I knew nothing about potty training, or anything! I was incredibly fortunate that she knew exactly what she was doing – or, certainly, she seemed to know. I had limited knowledge, but I never felt pushed out from that perspective. Dads can often feel that way, but it's still possible for us dads to play a huge role with our daughters.

A few years down the line, we were a family of seven, following the births, three years apart, of our daughters Saskia and Kendra. As my girls have grown, our relationships have just got better. They come to me with their problems and life issues, such as how to tax a car – all the "blue" jobs, as I call them – and I'm always there for that. We live in a world where some twenty years ago there were jobs for men and jobs for women, but I wanted my daughters to know they were capable of both. I consider my generation to be one of the first of men to be really hands-on with their children. We wanted to be there for our children.

Nowadays, there is an expectation on fathers that hasn't always been there; that men are emasculated in some way by being there for their children. As a young dad, I never felt that pressure. I just cared for my kids in the ways I wanted to. My own father, coming from an Italian background, was pretty hands on too, often cooking and always around. I never wanted to disappoint my parents, and they've always been supportive of me. I was lucky in that way – never having had high expectations placed on me. This is what I wanted to replicate with my daughters.

As a father, I can bring a sense of balance to my family. A female household can be fairly emotional, and I try to cut through that a little, particularly with their decision making. I try to encourage my girls not to make too many emotional decisions. A house of six women can be a weird place: amazing, so incredibly giving, offering a lot of emotional support – but also needing a lot of emotional support. I try to act as a brother to my daughters, as well as a dad. We have a laugh together, but I also offer guidance. I don't feel like I have to be the grown up all the time and, being a young dad, I feel fortunate to feel that way.

One of the hardest things is to be there for each daughter's needs, which are all different. I go from helping one daughter with a career change, to another through a

"In your heart, what do you want to do? Because that's what you need to follow."

LORENZO COLANGELO

relationship break-up. I try to deal with each one as and when needed, with each daughter in mind.

When the girls were younger, it was impossible to spend one-to-one time with them. We often went to dance classes as a family, to support them in their hobby, and so we were always together. I didn't place pressure on myself to make that time back then. It is certainly easier now to go for coffee and catch-ups than it was back then, and my girls' different personalities can shine through on these occasions.

My daughters have a strong bond with each other and I know they will turn to each other before they turn to me, which is so important. I think your behaviour as a parent will encourage that. We always reminded them that their sisters are their best friends, and they have all taken that on board.

I'm always proud of my daughters, but the standout things for me aren't so much the jobs they've got — it's about how they have adapted to change. During the Covid-19 lockdown, one of my daughters went for a job interview. She'd gone from West End star to supermarket worker through the pandemic, and she felt a little down about that change. I said to her, "More than any job you've ever got, this is the most proud of you I have ever been. You're putting pride to one side to do a job you feel you need to do." It's not about the stardom and the title. It's about the attitude you bring to what you do that defines you. To do the best they can do in any given moment is what makes me proud of my daughters.

I say to my daughters, "In your heart, what do you want to do? Because that's what you need to follow."

I give my daughters the permission to:

- *take an opportunity*
- *put their hands up*
- *not be afraid of change*

In return, they, alongside my wife, have given me so much support in pursuing what I want to do. As your children grow, they begin to appreciate what has got them so far, and mine have given so much back for that. We've seen a reversal of roles; they look out for me and make sure I'm okay. We're very lucky to have that relationship.

Having seen five daughters through their schooling now, I will admit I was a pretty rubbish help. Fortunately, my daughters all had the drive and the determination to do well. For me, exams have never been massive. I've never asked for exam results when interviewing. For an underachiever at school, I've done okay in life. I never put pressure on my daughters for this reason, and I never wanted grades to define who they were. Their work ethic was pretty good, and they all achieved good grades. I don't think I provided too much support, but I trusted my daughters to get on with it.

Teenage girls face a lot of challenges today. My advice would be to listen to them. When your daughter takes the time to talk with you and share her anxieties, you must take the time to listen, specifically at that moment. Nine times out of ten, my daughters will come to me, and I'll be preoccupied and half listen. I'm not proud of that, and I think it's important to give them your time when they need it. If now isn't the best time, remind yourself to give them that time later on in the day.

Don Miguel Ruiz is a spiritual teacher and author. He states that there are four agreements in being a good parent:

1. *Be impeccable with your word – what you say, and how you say it, is so important.*
2. *Don't take things personally; try to get over them quickly.*
3. *Don't make assumptions. Don't assume everything is okay.*
4. *Always do your best – be the best you can be in anything you do.*

As a parent, don't look for reassurances, and don't judge yourself. Don't put pressure on yourself to be the best parent. Just be the best you can be. Pretending everything is perfect will soon crash down because nothing is perfect. The perfect relationship reflects the good and bad. It's often hard to listen to your own advice, but it is important to look back and notice that. Show your children that not everything has been easy for you, and you've overcome your mistakes.

———

What I absolutely love the most about the contributors in this book is that I can bring you thoughts, ideas and wisdom not only from myself, but from others. I had never heard of Don Miguel Ruiz until Lorenzo opened my eyes to the four agreements mentioned above. It's ideas like these that I hope will give you the guidance you might be seeking for communicating with your daughter or a girl you know. I want to look at the four agreements in a little more detail so that together we can understand them better.

The four agreements offer a powerful code of conduct that Don Miguel Ruiz says can rapidly transform lives by offering a new experience of freedom, true happiness and love. The four agreements are based on ancient Toltec wisdom, which advocates freedom from self-limiting beliefs that may cause suffering and limitation in a person's life. The Toltec ruled central Mexico from the tenth to the twelfth century, and they were revered for their spiritual teachings. The word "Toltec", according to Ruiz, means "men and women of knowledge".

Agreement 1: Be Impeccable with Your Word

This agreement discusses avoiding hearsay, lies, empty promises and all the ways in which we cause problems with our words. Say only what you mean and realise that you can cause damage if you're not careful with your words.

Agreement 2: Don't Take Things Personally

This revolves around understanding how other people's behaviours are a reflection of them only. It is such a powerful message. We see this when someone is being unkind, or bullying, and often it's the person who's being unkind who has the issue, not the other way round. When someone gives us feedback about our behaviour or about us as an individual, it's important to remember that no opinions are truly objective; we all have our biases, our filters, through which we view the world. With this in mind, we shouldn't take anyone else's view of ourselves or our actions as entirely accurate.

When someone says something about us, they're really saying something about themselves and how they view the world.

Agreement 3: Don't Make Assumptions

It can cause unnecessary stress to constantly assume you know what other people are thinking. We shouldn't be making assumptions about what others are thinking without checking with them. Understanding that other people might have different reasons for their actions is important. We should try to understand others and consider their motivations before jumping to conclusions about their behaviour or choices. This thought process can really help prevent interpersonal conflict.

Agreement 4: Always Do Your Best

This is perhaps my favourite of the four agreements because we are constantly just asking our girls to do their best. If you do the best that you can at any time, then you can always be proud of yourself and have no regrets. We will all have good days and bad days, but as long as we're putting an honest effort into the things that we do, then we can hold our heads high and have nothing to feel ashamed of.

Seven Conversations to Have with Our Daughters About Putting Their Hands Up

Putting your hand up, and encouraging your daughter to put her hand up, isn't just about answering a question, it's about helping the next girl put her hand up, too. Our children become mini-mentors without even realising it. As your daughter raises her hand, she will become a role model for the other girls in the class, which can encourage the next girl to raise her hand too.

Our girls must not look down on their mistakes, they must look up and raise their hands. We all have a role to play in changing the look of leadership in our world and it starts by raising a hand. Here are some ways to discuss these important ideas with your daughter.

1. Talk to her about when she last raised her hand in class. If she tends to avoid it because she finds it scary, ask her why.

2. Explain that by putting her hand up, she will be showing her teacher that she really cares about doing well in class.

3. If she's worried about putting her hand up, tell her to take her time and write a few notes about what she wants to say before she says it out loud, so it doesn't fly out of her head.

4. Remind her to take a breath and relax so her thoughts are clear in her mind before she says them.

5. Tell her not to feel pressured to say the answer quickly. She should take the time to answer at a pace that is right for her.

6. Tell her to never be embarrassed by her answer. If it's partly right, then she has done a great job. If she gets it wrong, learn from it and move on.

7. Keep trying! Even if, at first, her words don't come out right, or she speaks quietly, over time, she'll find her voice. It gets easier with practice.

Conversation 2: "I can't do this. Other people do this."

I was speaking to a friend of mine about a girl she knew. The girl, in her early teens, was in her bedroom. She was sitting on the floor with her hands hugging her knees. She was in floods of tears. Her mum had gone into her bedroom to ask her to come down for dinner after she hadn't responded when her brother shouted up the staircase. When her mum asked what was wrong, she cried and said, "I feel under so much pressure. To be smart. To be pretty. To be good at everything. It's just so hard."

This girl's mind is telling her that society expects nothing short of perfection from her. Too many of our girls are trying so hard to meet the unhealthy, stereotypical expectations of being perfect – they are living in the shadow of what I call the myth of the perfect girl.

Many of us can relate to this situation, and it's so tough for a parent to witness. In fact, I have to be honest here, I had the most heart-wrenching conversation with my own daughter recently, who was also telling me that she feels pressure to be "perfect". The worrying thing is that she felt this way even before she had access to her own social media accounts. Could the pressure of perfection run deeper than social media?

I found it hard to write this page. I – the author of this book – am having to admit, in my own words, that perfectionism is an issue in my own home. Later on, my daughter told me that she didn't mean it; she said she wasn't sure why she'd said it. Even so, it's something I'll monitor, and it's not something I've forgotten. So, if I'm struggling to find the answers to this perfectionism pressure, perhaps you might be feeling the same too.

When we look at our young girls from the outside, we often see them excelling. We are so proud of them and everything they are doing. However, our girls sometimes see things differently. On the inside, they're on the verge of imploding. It's exhausting – and it's a big issue. When I realised this, I considered whether this is more of an issue for girls than boys. I have two sons. Do they also have unhealthy thoughts of perfection or is it more prevalent in girls? When I researched this, I struggled to find answers. Interestingly enough, when I ran an online search on the topic of perfection in *children*, the books that came up on the first page were mostly aimed at parents of daughters, with photos of girls on the front covers.

There's no reason why perfectionism should be gender specific. I think we all know people with perfectionist tendencies, and the thing about perfectionism is that it is cruel; it takes no prisoners. There's no room for error. This is what, sadly, can lead children to struggle with anxiety, depression and low self-esteem, and this is why it is important we address the subject.

There may not be a simple solution to these unhealthy thoughts of perfection, other than reminding our girls, often, about what is reality and what is not. Reality is that humans are imperfect and, in fact, the world is an imperfect place. There's always so much work to be done to improve who we are and the world we live in. One idea that could potentially help our girls deal with the pressure to be perfect is resilience, a topic we will talk more about later on. Of course, resilience doesn't guarantee that everything will be washed aside when things go wrong or when our girls are upset by their *imperfect* test scores. One of my friends was telling me how her daughter was upset that she got a result of 99 per cent on a test. It wasn't good enough. It wasn't perfect.

We probably don't talk enough about the subject of recovery with kids, but I think it's important. When sportspeople train – or when we do hard things – we need to give ourselves permission to recover. Building your daughter's resilience will give her a greater capacity for recovery, and encouraging the behavioural traits of adaptiveness and agility will help her to learn how to recover quicker when she encounters stress and challenges. We pause, we reset and we go again. Stronger every time, without the need for perfection. The most important aspect is that our girls are working towards *their* personal best, whatever their personal best looks like.

Seeking External Validation

Sometimes our girls seem to be looking for a tick-box validation of their worth, instead of nurturing their own strengths and values. This leads girls to work harder, but, equally, it often leaves them feeling as if they can never do enough. Perhaps this is the crucial point where the anxiety kicks in? When I spoke to Girlguiding UK about this, they told me that every year, one in four of us in the UK is affected by a mental health issue such as anxiety, so it's likely that you, or someone you know, will experience this at some point.

Hearing this from Girlguiding UK was a turning point for me because I felt this was a statistic that should not be ignored.

The number of people affected by an anxiety disorder around the world is equally high. In fact, by the time I've finished quoting statistics, there will be even more affected. The numbers are increasing all the time. *The Washington Post* reported that, according to the Census Bureau, one third of Americans now show signs of clinical anxiety or depression.

When it comes to our children, anxiety and depression are on the rise. Whether they personally suffer from these conditions or not, our teens are seeing significant problems among their peers. It surrounds us all. The PEW Research Center in the US says that when it comes to the pressures facing teens, school work tops the list: 61 per cent of teens say they feel a lot of pressure to get good grades. By contrast, 28–29 per cent say they feel a lot of pressure to look good and to fit in socially, while 21 per cent feel similarly pressured to be involved in extracurricular activities and to be good at sports.

While boys and girls face many of the same pressures – for example, they feel equal pressure to get good grades – the report shows that their daily experiences and pressures differ in other ways. Girls are more likely than boys to say they face a lot of pressure to look good, and a larger proportion of girls than boys say they often feel tense or nervous about approaching their day.

Further research from a 2020 annual report by the Center for Collegiate Mental Health summarised the state of college student mental health from US and international colleges. It found that anxiety and depression continued to be the most common concerns experienced by students during the 2018–19 academic year.

From my research, it seems one thing is for sure – self-confidence holds the key to unlocking some of these anxieties. Yet some girls have trouble finding self-confidence and keeping hold of it. Somehow, life feels a little more intense for the girls of today.

Am I pretty enough?

Am I smart enough?

Just the simple thought, *am I enough?*

These conversations are going on all over the world right now. The need for change and the need to support our girls has become so great that doing something about it became my main driver for this book.

With so many pressures around body image and the constant fear of what other people think about us, we need to have an honest conversation with our daughters about this. If there is one thing I have learnt for sure – it's that you may not be the prettiest, the most popular or the smartest girl in the class, but you'll always have the power to create your own world of happiness. We must squash the idea of the "perfect girl" because it's damaging our girls.

When I first considered writing a book, my immediate thoughts were... *Other people do this. Other people write books. What makes me worthy of being able to write a book?* And that made me question myself: *Why am I thinking whether or not I am worthy enough?* Is it because I know that getting a publishing contract is difficult and that sometimes, when things are difficult, we don't want to do them? Or maybe it's because when we show our work to other people, we know we're opening ourselves up to feedback – perhaps criticism – and the possibility that somebody will say, "This piece of work isn't good

You may not be
the prettiest, the
most popular or
the smartest girl
in the class, but
you'll always
have the power
to create your own
world of happiness.

enough." When we bring these thoughts together, the prospect of someone saying, "This isn't good enough," means that our minds sometimes tell us that we can't do it – even before we have tried.

But what if we *can*?

What if, as women and girls, we are prepared to take the feedback, to listen to constructive criticism and hear from those who say this piece of work isn't for them, or they don't feel it's good enough? What if we overcome the fear of failure or rejection and do it anyway?

Imagine there is someone out there who wants to take a chance on you. Because that's what happened to me – my literary agent, Jessica Killingley, and Stephanie Milner, the editor of this book! We can do it. But only if we really believe in it – and in ourselves. It starts by changing that inner dialogue we have with ourselves.

Around three years ago, when I told my daughter that, one day, I was going to write a book, she asked in return, "Who is the book for?" It was a great question. I told her that I wanted to write a book for parents and caregivers of girls. A book that helps girls be their best, confident selves. She turned around and said, "I think that sounds really cool, Mum." And with that, I started writing. However, she also needs to know about the *many* publishing houses who politely declined my work before the one that said yes.

I persevered and I achieved my goal in the end. But it made me wonder if we have undervalued the importance of showing our girls how to use failure as feedback. If we teach our girls *how* to be persistent, perhaps that could help them too. Could this be a game changer?

An Ordinary Girl Who Became Extraordinary

Not that it's good to categorise people, but I would say that I was an ordinary student. As secondary school progressed, life delivered a bitter blow. My parents were getting divorced. So, as I was sitting my GCSE exams, I found myself living away from home with my aunt and uncle. They were very kind to me, but my home and school life became confusing and disrupted. I even missed a couple of exams because no one took me to school to sit them, so I was already behind on my overall GCSE results. I know it was a difficult time for my parents too, and they tried to shield us three children from as much of the pain as possible. On reflection, and now as a parent of three children myself, it must have been an extremely painful time for both of my parents.

When I telephoned the school to get my GCSE results, one of my teachers answered the phone. She told me that I got a C-grade in French. She went on to tell me that she was "disappointed" because she felt I was capable of "*better*". It's unlikely she was aware of my personal situation, but it was one of the first times that I truly felt like a failure. No one likes to hear the word "disappointment". But sometimes, someone telling us something negative can spur us on to want to do something positive – to challenge that opinion. Maybe that was the moment I decided I wanted to be an ordinary girl who would achieve something extraordinary.

Instead of going to drama college at age sixteen, as I'd planned, I gave up the opportunity in favour of going into business with my brother, Richard, who was four years older than me. At the time, perhaps it felt like a way to escape college, which I wasn't particularly enjoying. But whatever my motives were, I did something *brave*. I shot my hand up into the air and gave something new a go when I had no expectations of where that journey may lead.

Some twenty years on, my brother and I still run that company together. Crazy, right? It has grown into a global, award-winning mobile tech company called Active Digital, with a multi-million pound turnover. I love being a woman in tech. It all started from that teacher telling me I was a disappointment. That was the turning point that pushed me to rebel against her expectations and work my hardest.

Our years in education bring out so many different emotions in us all. Many of us would have met lifelong friends in our school days. Many of us have plenty of magical moments we remember fondly. However, many girls experience tough times in school and come out with memories they would prefer to forget. As parents and caregivers, we need to be there to listen to the good and the bad. More than anything, I think of our school years as a place where we first start to experience setbacks and what we consider failures.

Now I sit here with a daughter of my own, and we chat about the good days and the not so good days, the days when a friendship has gone wayward or situations when she feels like she has failed. I try to guide her and give her the tools to see how she can use these failures as a learning experience. I gently remind her that she never fails – she only learns.

F – First
A – Attempt
I – In
L – Learning

I was a confident kid. That doesn't necessarily mean I was loud or would eagerly throw myself into new challenges, but it meant I was happy enough to give different things a try. My mum reminds me that I was quiet, content and well-behaved as a child. Well-behaved most of the time, that is, when I wasn't chopping off my little brother's fringe and getting lost in the woods with him while picking wild flowers. All in all, I was generally well-behaved and I didn't seem to cause her too much trouble. In fact, considering my positive and expressive exterior, it has taken me a jolly long time to find my voice. In finding my voice, I have worked hard to grow into my own sense of self and throw aside any urges for perfectionism.

The confidence journey is a long one. I'm sure many of you reading this book may have had people in your life who've tried to knock the wind out of your sails: from people telling you that you're not good at certain things, to people telling you you're overweight; the list goes on.

It's common for us to suffer from a lack of self-confidence at some point during our lives. There is a difference between confidence and self-confidence. In general, confidence refers to something external: your abilities, your actions and other people's as well. Self-confidence, however, more specifically refers to confidence in oneself – believing in yourself, in your opinions and feelings, and accepting and celebrating those things. Self-confidence is believing in your inner voice. It can give our girls that much needed source of inner strength and conviction, enabling them to grow their confidence so they can overcome obstacles and achieve their goals.

Many of us, particularly women and girls, are good at focusing on self-critical thoughts, whether they are about our looks, our skills or our bodies. We are often our own worst critics. Last summer on holiday, my daughter came up to me and hugged my stomach. "You are so beautiful, Mummy." It was in that moment I realised that whatever was going on in my head about my own body confidence or fears about what I looked like in my swimming costume, here was my daughter, standing in front of me, telling me I was beautiful. It was right then that I realised I was her role model… and she was mine.

I've since realised that although I care deeply what people think of me (it's my nature), I've learnt to like myself a little more. I remind myself to focus on what makes me happy because, although it might sound like a cliché, being happy – and ensuring our children are happy – is the most important thing.

Confidence and self-belief play such an important role in our daily lives, and no one ever tells us that the confidence journey is a long one. If you see a woman who is rocking her confidence, you could be mistaken for thinking she may have clicked her fingers to make that happen. However, the more likely story is that her confidence has built up over her life, much the same as mine has.

Mindset is Everything

A girl's mindset plays a critical role in how she will cope with life's challenges. We all experience moments of self-doubt and uncertainty. Even the most confident among us still have moments when we think, "I'm such a failure." It's part of being human. When facing problems, girls who adopt a positive mindset will tend to show greater resilience. Whether you're talking about school, career success, starting your own business or getting through a tough period of your life, having the right mindset can make the biggest difference between success and failure.

American psychologist Dr Carol Dweck defined two types of mindset: a fixed mindset and a growth mindset. A fixed mindset assumes that our intelligence, character and creative ability are static – "fixed". Those with a fixed mindset find it very difficult to change or to believe they can better themselves. Believing that our own qualities can't be improved means we never will reach even a tiny part of our full potential. A growth mindset, on the other hand, allows us to see that we can improve through personal growth. It allows us to believe that when we cultivate our skills, we change and grow through our efforts.

You would think, wouldn't you, that surely everyone would want to have a growth mindset? But sadly, many don't feel that way. I shudder at the thought of the number of girls out there, globally, whose minds feel static. They're so afraid of trying something new or different in case they fail that they simply don't ever try. These girls have missed a huge point here – that failing is a form of learning. Failure is hardly ever to your detriment; most of the time, it's simply a springboard for self-improvement, for moving forward.

During my research, I came across the psychologist Abraham Maslow, one of the most influential psychologists of the twentieth century. He was driven by a passion to help people live the best lives they could, acknowledging their unique humanity along the way.

Among his most influential work was his contribution to humanistic psychology, as well as his development of the hierarchy of needs. I want to take a good look at the hierarchy of needs, which Maslow developed to understand what motivates us.

Maslow created a pyramid of five basic human needs, which he defined as: physiological, safety, love and belonging, esteem and self-actualisation. A person must broadly satisfy the needs of each level in order to be able to progress to the next.

You will notice that, when arranging the pyramid, Maslow placed the physiological needs at the bottom. These are the need for water, food and sleep, all of which are all basic requirements for us to live. Maslow defined the bottom four levels as "deficiency needs" – needs that arise from a lack of something. The top level, self-actualisation, is defined as a "growth need" – the desire for personal growth, the desire for *more*.

Only once all of the other needs of the pyramid have been met, can our girls achieve self-actualisation – the ability to be the best version of themselves. Maslow's theory is that to develop as a person, you must climb the pyramid, satisfying the lower levels along the way. Only when we reach the top can we fulfil our potential. Let's take a look at the five levels in more detail.

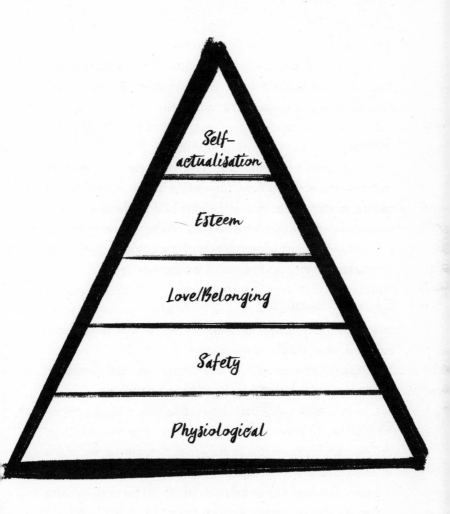

Maslow's hierarchy of needs takes the form of a pyramid, with the most basic needs at the bottom and the more complex and sophisticated needs at the top.

Physiological

These are the basic requirements for human survival. For example, food, drink, shelter, clothing and sleep. Maslow believed that if these basic needs are not met, then the human body can't function optimally.

Safety

Once the physiological needs have been met, the need for security and safety is next. This can relate to safety in your family, environment or community, and it's the basis of the importance of police, schools and medical care. However, other things to consider at this level are emotional security, financial security and personal wellbeing.

Love and Belonging

After the physiological and safety needs have been fulfilled, the third level on the pyramid is love and belonging. The need for friendship and all kinds of interpersonal relationships motivates behaviour.

Esteem

As we climb closer to the top of the pyramid, we reach esteem. Maslow believed people need to feel valued by others. The need for esteem plays a pivotal role in motivating our behaviour, turning "I can't" into "I can". People embrace the feeling of accomplishment, no matter how big or small, and recognise that when their efforts are praised, their self-esteem and self-worth grow.

Self-Actualisation

At the peak of Maslow's pyramid lies self-actualisation. Maslow believes this is the pinnacle of what people need in order to achieve their full potential as human beings. Maslow placed self-actualisation at the peak of human psychology because it can only be achieved when all other needs are satisfied. I like Maslow's definition of self-actualisation: "It may be loosely described as the full use and exploitation of talents, capabilities, potentialities, etc. Such people seem to be fulfilling themselves and to be doing the best that they're capable of doing. They are people who have developed or are developing to the full stature of which they are capable."

What I love about Maslow's theory is that it shows how important it is to recognise that personal growth is an amazing thing. The more our girls focus on self-worth and personal growth, the more they can silence the inner critic, and the better they can get at quieting the voices of those who wish to criticise theirs, or those who wish to make them feel small.

Of course, just like all theories out there, not everyone agrees that Maslow's hierarchy of needs is the be-all and end-all of human psychology, but we can all agree that raising girls with a healthy dollop of self-esteem and the desire for self-improvement will go a long way. Remember, growth needs don't stem from a lack of something, but rather from wanting to grow as a person.

I spoke to Ruth Cooper-Dickson who has a MSc (Master of Science degree) in Applied Positive Psychology and Coaching Psychology. The founder of Champs, a wellbeing consultancy, Ruth has worked with almost 400 teenage girls as part of the #ThisGirlCan programme. I have always found Ruth to be a great listener, which is probably why she spends so much time educating young people on the importance of mental wellbeing. Wellbeing is strongly connected to psychology, and it is psychologists who work hard to understand how humans work. Therefore, I wanted to find out what Ruth has learnt from spending time with so many girls, and what her advice is about how we can protect their mental wellbeing.

———

All Girls Can
by Ruth Cooper-Dickson

In 2016, I was invited to go into a few secondary schools in my home county of Derbyshire and deliver workshops as part of a campaign for #ThisGirlCan. I was going to be addressing nearly 400 teenagers, mostly girls, on the importance of a healthy mind.

Something I had noticed was how young girls today seem to have no clear goals in life. My personal childhood dream of becoming an English teacher or an actress gave me drive, something I feel is incredibly important, along with believing that you have the potential to make it anywhere. My #ThisGirlCan journey began with the aim of eliminating the mentality that leads to a lack of ambition, and presenting young girls at school with my personal story: through tough childhood times, to overcoming anxiety, to founding Champs.

In delivering workshops to schoolgirls as part of the #ThisGirlCan campaign, I discuss reframing negative thoughts and turning them into positive behaviours. I encourage girls to open up about the challenges they, as young females, are facing today. With a keen focus on self-esteem, wellbeing and positive behaviour for younger teens, and goal setting, resilience and coping with pressure for older students, I mostly educate girls on how they can work on not only their mental wellbeing, but how they can support the wellbeing of others around them too. I think that the teenage years for girls are all about "finding their feet", learning how to be themselves, to be unique and what that looks like.

I'm very committed to supporting the young girls of today and encouraging the growth of confident, positive young adults. Though I'll admit working with teens is often tough, and the engagement is not always there, I am constantly reassured by positive feedback, and the occasional "Thanks, Miss!" I think lack of confidence in young girls today may be a contributor to their lack of engagement in the classroom. I have come to the conclusion that girls are often afraid to admit they're good at something – some are even afraid to admit they enjoyed something!

I believe everybody is good at something. But, within a cohort of teenage girls, many are unable to identify just three talents, skills or traits they're good at. The heartbreaking reality can be seen in most of my workshops. On one particular occasion, we had a sheet of A4 paper, listing lots of different skills, such as cooking, football, rugby, etc. – traits too, like kindness and being a good friend. In groups, students had to identify which traits they held and identify those their friends held too. It turns out, teens can do this for their friends, but hardly any teens admitted they were good at anything! There's this fear of saying, "I'm good at that," or, "I want to have a go at that." I think that's really sad, and that's why #ThisGirlCan is so important. It says, "Have a go! You don't always have to be the best to enjoy something."

"We need to encourage our girls that simply trying and having fun is what's important. Don't fret on past mistakes; don't worry about being perfect."

RUTH COOPER-DICKSON

I often suggest that there's this trait most men seem to possess innately — they think they're good at something, even when they may not be. But women don't think this way, and often a woman will turn down an opportunity, or not put herself forward, because she doesn't think she holds all the traits she may need to succeed. I think we all need to take a tip from the men of the world and wing it a little bit more! Be good at something, but you don't need to be the best. Perfectionism creeps into our bones.

Personally, I can proudly state that I'm certainly not the perfectionist I used to be, more often settling for an "it's fine as it is" approach nowadays. Achieving this more relaxed frame of mind has taken me a long time, but it has been absolutely worth the effort; I'm no longer beating myself up after an email typo or taking that run a little slower.

I think girls are taught to be good at something, hence they are rewarded for the achievement, and not for simply trying something new, or for giving everything a go. But I say, so what if the run was slower? At least you went! We need to stop rewarding girls just for conforming to the norms, for fitting in or for being excellent at one specific talent. Instead, it's important to reward them for simply trying.

In my approach to teenage girls' body image and self-esteem issues, I normally see a great deal of judgement built into girls who are so young and impressionable. With social media now hotter than ever, and the well-known "Instagram versus reality" concept, girls today are expecting too much of themselves, and maybe even of others. We need to encourage our girls that simply trying and having fun is what's important. Don't fret on past mistakes; don't worry about being perfect.

Ruth's words of wisdom have really helped cement my strong opinion on how everybody is good at something. However, finding that "something" takes effort, confidence and bravery. Sometimes just taking the first step is all we need to start feeling braver and giving things a go. I will have to confess to Ruth at some point that the work she does with groups of students to help them identify which traits they hold, is something I now do myself, when I speak to groups of students. I hope she'll take this as a compliment! If you ask someone to write down three things they are good at, it's incredibly interesting to see the results. Of the hundreds of students with whom I've completed this worksheet, only a small number managed to write down three things. Yet they find it very easy to write down three positive things about a friend. Internalising our own strengths and abilities is the biggest hurdle.

Ruth said to me that for teens, there's so much going on to make sense of. Often, saying something out loud for the first time can be frightening – it validates it, makes it real. Considering that we are discussing the conversation that begins with your daughter saying, "I can't do this!", I'm strongly reminded how important that self-confidence barrier is. My self-confidence fluctuates all the time, so I imagine the same applies to our girls. One minute they're drowning in confidence and the next minute you might find that someone says something in passing that completely crushes their confidence in one fell swoop. Without doubt, this has happened to me many times. The important part is how we learn to get back up again – how we rebuild the confidence and have those crucial, internal, positive conversations with ourselves.

Self-confidence starts when we try to have better self-awareness and when we are able to celebrate our own strengths and abilities. This book isn't about teaching your daughter how to conquer the world. It's about finding an honest approach to help your daughter understand herself and her own strengths and learn how to applaud them without needing to be "perfect". This book is about me helping to teach you how to develop more confident girls.

Confidence is key to how we approach new situations or challenges – from our first job interview to meeting new people in socially busy situations. Some people thrive on being in busy environments, having to make a speech or making small talk with new people, but for others this can be incredibly daunting.

Growing your confidence can be tricky, but Philippa Gogarty and Anna Gibson, the co-founders of Micro Scooters, had to do exactly that as they grew their business. Making decisions, taking opportunities and having a positive mindset have helped them do it. Philippa and Anna founded Micro Scooters in the UK back in 2004 after spotting a scooter in their local park. Anna's two-year-old son had a go on the flashy-looking scooter and was hooked. Philippa and Anna signed the UK and Ireland distribution rights for Micro Scooters and, from there, the business has boomed. I asked Philippa, as a mother of a daughter herself, how she would pass on what she has learnt in growing a hugely successful business. Was it all down to confidence? I wanted to know what she does to encourage her daughter, Georgia, to learn through new experiences, and she told me about how, if we want to raise confident girls, we need to continually "check in" with them and stand by them.

———

We Need to Listen and Trust
by Philippa Gogarty

I remember this little girl that always knew her own mind and had a complex set of characteristics. Despite being so young, she was always determined and focused. I wouldn't say she was the most confident or outgoing child, but she knew what she wanted. Because she has younger siblings, she has always felt a sense of responsibility. I think that's quite common when you're the eldest.

By the time Georgia was six or seven, she was self-contained and often stubborn. She was always part of a bright, competent group at primary school. She's always been fiercely competent and would one day, I think, make a good leader. I have a distinct memory of driving with her to Battersea Park when she was thirteen for a photoshoot for Micro Scooters, and we didn't have a licence for the photoshoot. It was Georgia who, whilst I drove the car and directed her, contacted the council and managed to negotiate a temporary licence.

In most cases, we see that confidence grow in our children over the years, and in Georgia's case, her confidence has developed through experience. I remember her phoning before her history GCSE exam, in tears about not being able to remember anything. She didn't believe in herself, even though she went on to gain an A* grade. Proof that even when we have worked really hard, we still find it difficult to believe we can achieve.

Looking back, I was over-concerned with Georgia's

apparent obsession with clothes and makeup. I thought it was superficial. However, I now realise it was an immature expression of an interest in creativity. I'm visually motivated, and Georgia was expressing a part of herself that would later develop into an intuitive love for and understanding of marketing, as well as for visual and written communication.

I always try to tell mothers of teenage girls who seem obsessed with seemingly superficial things, like their looks or makeup, that this might be a passion. Don't be scared that clothing or makeup brands will define them because often that's not what it's about. Try not to make them feel guilty for expressing this part of themselves. Try to channel their creativity and let them express themselves rather than fight it. This is all a natural part of growing up.

Girls come in all emotional shapes and sizes, with lots of varying characteristics. They can be complicated, but this shouldn't be prejudged. Get on the same side as your teenage daughters. This doesn't have to mean having a lot to say to them, often it's more a case of just being there. It's worth remembering you aren't always there as a friend; it is more important to be there as a parent. You'll go through periods when there are awkward silences, but creating these moments are vital. Always having an evening meal together, or some family time together, despite the silences, is key. Children need accessibility to us as parents, confidence that we'll always be there. Even at older ages, people often revert back to how they were at home. Don't expect to be their friend all the time. Sometimes those difficult times are just part of the journey.

"We have raised our children to have open conversations and to challenge the norm."

PHILIPPA GOGARTY

Try to work out if an expression of frustration with you is actually about a friend or something from school. Stay close. Try to talk while the pressure isn't on, for example, while driving, cooking or walking. Empathise and tell your daughter how you manage your friends. No one is perfect, so suspend your judgement and just listen before you give advice. Listening is key. Most of the time they have the answer themselves and they know what they need to say to their friends – so trust them!

No one and perhaps nothing can prepare us for parenting. It's one of the hardest roles we play. The feeling of not being good enough is ever present. However, as long as you provide a safe place for her, and love, you are doing a good enough job. Children go through phases. Trust them. Bring them up to be open minded. We have raised our children to have open conversations and to challenge the norm.

If you want to raise a resilient girl, then keep checking in with them and stand alongside them. Having the conversations, and the confidence in yourself to set the boundaries of when it's mum and daughter time, family time or time for yourself is important. Now my daughter is in her mid-twenties; she makes me so proud and I'm as grateful for her support as she is for mine.

———

Philippa has touched on the subject of listening to our daughters, so I want to expand on that and talk about active listening. Active listening is creating a space where you aren't thinking about how to respond to the speaker's question, not even trying to pre-empt the other person's thoughts or wondering what's for dinner tonight. It's when you are just in the moment, and deeper than the moment.

According to Ruth Cooper-Dickson, active listening requires a sense of connection and empathic response. It seems like a skill many of us would benefit from learning. The more we try to actively listen to our daughters, the more I hope they will feel they can speak to us – freely and relaxed. Ruth says that, as a mental health first-aider coach, she will often sit, for ten minutes or so, with a client in silence – which takes a lot of patience. But by not filling in the gaps, people will eventually say something. One-to-one active listening can prove really powerful.

Ruth says that active listening is about seeking to understand before being understood. Her top tip for practising active listening with your daughter is to "walk and talk". Walking, with no interruptions, and no one else around. This allows for calmness, creativeness, space and most importantly, equality. When you walk side-by-side, neither one of you is of greater importance. This is so essential!

As Philippa has so well described, our daughters seem to change into young adults so quickly. As your daughter changes, it's important that your relationship with her grows and evolves at the same time to meet her needs. You may find yourself looking to adopt new ways to connect with her again. Change with her.

We talk about raising confident, happy girls as though it's achievable. I do not believe that anyone is confident and happy all the time. However, it is our ability to express vulnerability and reach out when we're feeling overwhelmed that creates resilience and wellbeing. Our role is to guide our daughters to find their own paths and rhythms. Help her forget perfection and focus on loving herself. The teenage years are a great transition for our girls. Together, we can help them to grow, adapt and achieve. Together, we can raise them well.

Philippa Gogarty's Top Seven Characteristics of a Self-Confident Girl

Although some girls will use false confidence to mask their insecurities, true self-confidence has a look all its own. Self-confidence starts on the inside; being happy with who they are and what they do is a critical part of confidence for our girls. Using these seven characteristics that Philippa has laid out, you and your daughter can, together, work towards these goals. Do any of the following describe your daughter? Which ones can you work on together, and how?

1. **She is able to ask for help when she needs it.**

2. **She has faith in her own decisions.**

3. **She is independent but recognises her need to rely on others.**

4. **She understands positive body image.**

5. **She pursues her own interests and passions.**

6. **She believes in herself.**

7. **She knows she is good enough.**

Conversation 3: "I really messed up today – what am I going to do?"

I have been thinking a lot about building bravery in girls. Recently, my daughter was playing rugby, which she does most weekends. She came home with a swollen knee, to which I applied a bag of frozen peas. I sent a text message to her coach, Lee, and thanked him for looking after Erin after quite a tough tackle. He replied to me saying, "No problem. Erin played with no fear today." I had never really considered myself a parent of a daughter who is fearless. I contemplated what the difference was between bravery and fearlessness? Would you say that being brave is being strong in the face of fear, while fearlessness is being free from fear?

One of my favourite TED Talks focuses on the topic of raising brave girls. It is a talk by Caroline Paul, a firefighter, paraglider and author of *The Gutsy Girl: Escapades for Your Life of Epic Adventure*. In Caroline's TED Talk she opens up the conversation on our society's tendency to encourage timid behaviour in girls. Caroline talks about a research project that studied the dynamics of a playground where there was a fire pole. Researchers found that mums and dads were very likely to warn their daughters about the risks of playing on the fire pole and were more likely to assist them on it. On the other hand, boys were encouraged by their parents to play on the fire pole despite any trepidation, and these boys were given guidance on how they could use the fire pole independently. The message was clear: girls should be fearful while boys should be brave!

Everyone will have their own opinions on this, but the point Caroline is making is that we shouldn't treat girls and boys differently in this way because it reinforces that girls should be timid while boys should be fearless. We need our girls to find confidence in themselves and to make decisions that make them feel strong, brave or perhaps – as in my daughter's case – fearless. I wonder if some of us are born more fearless than others. Are some of us just more self-assured than others? Experts say that children are born with a neutral sense of themselves, which means that how our girls are raised, socialisation and other factors play a significant part in either building confidence or tearing it down.

When I go into schools, I talk to the girls about the importance of raising their hands. Sometimes it takes a girl to feel just a tiny bit braver that day to make a small change. Raising a hand today is about being braver today than you were yesterday. You might wonder why this is so important. Even today in business, only a few women might raise their hand in a meeting. This is because they were probably not encouraged to do this as a child. That's why it is so important to do this small act of bravery now. This is how we find our next leaders, creators, thinkers and doers. This is how we change the world and make history at the same time. Leadership takes bravery, and it is built over a lifelong journey of courage and commitment.

So, how do we encourage girls to try something new if they have a constant fear of messing up? From a young age, girls are told to "stay in line", and when we ask girls to follow those simple sets of rules, it leaves no room for error. Our girls grow up feeling that they can't take risks or try new things, just in case it goes wrong… and they will fall outside the line. Then what?

The frustrating thing here is that we know that to grow as individuals, we have to push through the boundaries. We have to try new things and we have to be prepared that it might not work out, which can be a hard pill to swallow at times. The fear of messing up may be keeping our girls safe, but it fills them with anxiety and suffocates their capabilities. Our girls are selling themselves short because they're too afraid to take a chance.

What if I fail?

But what if you spectacularly succeed?

Taking Risks

With pressure mounting on our girls, some days it feels as if there is a constant fear of messing up. Perhaps the potentially toxic demands of social media and exams are causing our girls to feel so much worry and anxiety. I'm sure you have your thoughts on this. I know it's a monster topic. Sometimes it feels as though we all live in a world where we are not allowed to mess up. Even whilst writing this book, it slowly dawned on me that maybe I have perfectionist tendencies too. Before I had even started, I was worried that not every sentence or chapter would be "just so". Naturally, I kept most of those feelings internalised. I didn't tell anyone that I wanted it to be perfect. I just typed out sentences and deleted them when I felt they weren't "good enough".

The pressures today for girls to not mess up can be overwhelming, and, in some cases, can seem to control every aspect of their lives. Whether it's posting Instagram photos, getting the highest grades, landing prized scholarships or getting into the best universities, it's exhausting. Not just for the girls, but for us too.

I do voluntary work with Girlguiding UK and, since 2009, they have been giving girls and young women (aged 11–21) a platform on which to speak out on the issues that matter to them. In the 2019 Girlguiding UK survey, a third of girls aged 7–10 said they believe that they are judged on their appearance. A quarter of those felt that they need to be *perfect*.

When it comes to exams, nearly two-thirds of girls and young women who responded to the Girlguiding UK survey said there was too much pressure and focus on doing well in exams. Our girls are worried that not achieving high grades will ruin their future chances. However, as we have already learnt, we can achieve so much without always having the A-grades on a piece of paper. Angela Salt, CEO of Girlguiding UK says, "There are persistent issues for girls that just aren't going away. The combination of specific pressures and challenges girls face, because they are girls, stops them reaching their potential and enjoying life to the full. And that's wrong. At Girlguiding, we want to help to change this and support girls to thrive."

When it comes to risk, it's understandable that we want to keep our girls away from it, since they're the most precious things in our lives. But risk, as we know, is important to help us understand how to undertake the challenges life will throw at us. Our parents and grandparents will kindly remind us of the world they grew up in, where children were self-reliant and "tough".

So, in today's world, *are* we overprotecting our children? Have we taken it a step too far? Nowadays we have playgrounds where the fast roundabouts are gone and the floors are covered with bouncy rubber surfacing. Have we gone too far?

Several years ago, teachers at the Richmond Avenue Primary and Nursery School in Shoeburyness, UK, looked at their school campus critically and set about to "safely" bring in risk. Out went the plastic playhouses. The playground instead got a mud pit, a tyre swing, log stumps and workbenches with hammers. "We thought, how can we bring that element of risk into your everyday environment?" said Leah Morris, who manages the early years' programme at the school.

When it comes to taking everyday risks, should we stop trying to eliminate these for our girls? Is Leah Morris right? For parents, risk is an everyday dilemma. If cushioned, soft playgrounds were a metaphor for life, it would be an interesting one, because unfortunately life isn't really like that. It's little wonder that our girls are growing up afraid to take risks when, at times, we're so scared of letting them live for themselves.

Of course, my heart skips a beat when my kids want to climb trees, but is that not just part of being a parent? Play is how our children learn. Through play, they have the opportunity to express themselves. But, I wonder how they can do that, if we, as adults, are there directing them all the time? Direction gives them no freedom for imaginative play. I'm not saying that we should sit back and let kids do whatever they want (that's just asking for trouble!) but, from what we're learning here, is overprotective parenting holding our children back from learning to be independent? Will they end up growing up not knowing how to take risks?

Should we listen to the saying, "Don't prepare the road of life for your children, prepare your children for the road"? We hear about parents who pay extra for their child's scores or grades to be changed on college entrance applications, thinking they're doing their child a favour. But are they really?

Experience can be a Great Teacher

No matter how old our children are, sometimes, when they do something wrong – when they mess up or don't get the grade they want – our first reaction is to *fix it*. This may seem simple, but it starts with toys. They break them, we fix them. When it comes to their homework, they make a mistake, we rub it out with an eraser as if it never happened.

Interestingly enough, at my daughter's school, erasers aren't permitted. They can cross out their answer if they want to change it, but it will always be visible. The school said they wanted the students to see their mistakes and to acknowledge them. It made me wonder how many other schools use the same method.

On further research, it would seem that our school isn't the only one to use this method. Cognitive scientist Guy Claxton says, "The eraser is an instrument of the devil because it perpetuates a culture of shame about error. It's a way of lying to the world, which says 'I didn't make a mistake. I got it right the first time.' That's what happens when you can rub it out and replace it."

Professor Claxton goes on to say that schools should encourage students to acknowledge their mistakes because that's the way the big wide world works, and we should move away from placing too much importance on grades. We need a culture where children aren't afraid to make mistakes. They should look at their mistakes and learn from them, continuously reflecting and improving on what they've done, and not being pressured to get the right answer quickly so they can look smart. I think Guy and I would get on rather well if we ever met. I love how he too believes that it is indeed resilience and curiosity that are two essential ingredients for pupil success.

When children are young, parents typically spend time directing their behaviour. However, as children enter the teenage years, a parent's role ideally shifts to coaching their children, along with helping them make their own decisions and accept personal responsibility. As a parent myself, I recognise that it's so hard to see them mess up. Our natural instinct is to rescue them. It pains me to say this, but we must let them mess up. Sometimes they have to experience the consequences of their choices. Experience can be a great teacher even when sometimes it's tough to witness.

So how can we help?

I spoke to two contributors for this chapter, who were both very keen to help on this topic. The first is Lauren Derrett, mother of four, stepmother of two, with twenty-four years of parenting under her belt. Lauren seemed like a great person to offer some advice here. She left school at fourteen, before trying lots of different jobs. Lauren is an entrepreneur, the founder of the successful business, Wear 'em Out, a reusable period-pads company for the empowered eco-curious. Lauren has proved that you can give yourself permission to mess up, pick yourself back up and carry on. It's such a joy to watch Lauren running her business around her family, and I am so pleased she was happy to contribute to this book.

Before we dive into her words of wisdom, I want to talk about what I love about her company, Wear 'em Out. Firstly, Lauren is doing an amazing job in opening up the conversation on periods. Often considered a taboo subject, this is something we need to discuss more with our girls. Lauren was concerned about the amount of waste produced by menstrual products. Wear 'em Out reusable period pads are more sustainable than disposable tampons or pads, which can take up to 800 years to degrade. More than 4.3 billion disposable menstrual products are used in the UK every year, equating to 200,000 tonnes of menstrual waste hitting UK landfill per year. With Lauren's organisation, not only is she helping the environment, but she's also using her voice to speak out on an important topic: periods. Who knew that someone could make period pads cool? But somehow, she has absolutely nailed it.

Help Them Find Their Way
by Lauren Derrett

I hated school. I moved and changed schools and, to be honest, the new school people were not my people. I tried to build friendships for over a year, but it was tough. I felt like I didn't fit in.

Back then, I didn't have the support around me, and I was often left to my own devices. My mum once said to me, "I'm going to drag you to school by your hair," and I just replied, "Go on then." Nothing fazed me, and in my view, I think that was a blessing in disguise. A lot of people aren't comfortable saying, "I give up, I'm moving on," – but I am. I've never had a career, I've never excelled at anything, because I don't stick around long enough.

There's something inbuilt in me that if something doesn't feel right, I move on. And so, at age fourteen, I made a decision to leave school.

After leaving school, things were not easy and I sofa-surfed for a while. At one point I was homeless. I managed to carve out a job for myself as a qualified hairdresser because I didn't know what else to do. By the age of eighteen, things finally started to settle down for me.

I got a flat with my sister and got a new job working as a full-time nanny. On reflection, I see now that I probably had a need to be a mother because I wasn't well-mothered myself, so becoming a nanny felt like a natural transition. After working for a while, I met my husband and, by the age of twenty-three, I had a baby of my own. I was soon happily married with three children and was living the life I saw everyone else living. However, that didn't mean that I was always happy within myself. I can honestly say that it has taken me until now, at age forty-six to finally say I'm ready to become the best version of me. I'm ready.

Hand on heart, I'm so happy with who I am, I want to push myself further and further to see just how good I can be! If I push myself, through exercise and challenging myself business-wise, I feel I can be brilliant. I want to fulfil and make my own success story. It took me until now to realise this, but imagine how brilliant it can be if girls in their teens can push themselves to realise their self-worth now!

My lack of qualifications definitely led to a feeling of lack of worth. To me, grades mean nothing. I have survived without them. However, for my daughter, at sixteen years old, they mean a lot to her. I try to teach her that grades don't define you and, overall, they don't show who you are, but I agree, good grades can certainly propel you into great things.

Watching my daughter navigate this world as a young woman, I often think that she's going to have to fight for her place. Personally, I think we're miles away from equality, with regards to academia and domestic load. I'm not sure that will ever be balanced out. It's hard watching her grow because of the world we live in.

Showing my daughter my true self is so important. I show her I'm weak sometimes and that I have emotions. In equal measure, I also show her that I believe in myself and I know I'm enough. She now often recognises her emotions, and she knows when she's feeling confident or when she's lacking self-worth, which is so important because she's growing into such a strong woman.

There is a real deficit of self-worth in young girls, which we need to target. There is that fear of failure. A fear of judgement.

Shame is such a powerful emotion, and it resides in all of us regardless of anything. The problem with shame is that it grows in the dark — and that's something I learnt the hard way. The best way to treat shame is to "out" it and shine a light on it. You want to detach from it, so that shame becomes something outside of you, rather than being a part of you. You can go through experiences that you attach shame to, and the longer you hide that shame and keep it to yourself, the bigger it grows. The experiences we go through don't need to be part of who we are. And so, I dump my shame. In my book Filter Free, *I wanted to create a platform for others to do the same, and it has worked; it has encouraged just that.*

With the emotion of shame, those feelings don't go anywhere. They grow in you and distort your beliefs in yourself. By confiding in someone else, or simply writing it down in a journal, you get that shame out and leave it behind. What you're feeling isn't who you are − it's just a feeling. For everything you hold inside your head, you're not leaving room for new stuff. Eventually you'll be so muddled up with stuff that you won't be able to function − so get the bad stuff out! Whenever your head feels full, write, draw, sing, shout in a field or find an outlet that works for you. Free yourself from those stories that weigh you down. What happened yesterday is just a story now. And what happens in the future is just your imagination. Neither is real right now.

As a mother of a teenage daughter, my main advice to parents and caregivers is to let your teen believe they're doing it their own way − and give them that space and respect to do so. The hardest thing for any parent is to watch your child fall over. But it's paramount, because that falling over will lead to them coming back stronger and gaining confidence in themselves. It's important to let our kids feel everything, but give them the tools to be able to deal with the things they're feeling. I don't hide things from my kids − yes, all this bad stuff happens − but I

"Eventually you'll be so muddled up with stuff that you won't be able to function – so get the bad stuff out!"

LAUREN DERRETT

model the tools I have used to overcome it. My main advice is to allow your kid to fall apart, but teach them why we need an outlet to help when they do fall apart, and how that can look. We then need to give our kids the tools to help fix their problems, instead of solving the problems ourselves. Because those tools will last them forever.

Respect your kids. This is their journey. You may not agree with what they do, but they need to learn in their own way. The hardest part about having kids is not always believing in the same things as them. But they're growing up to have their own independence, and that's really important. As parents and caregivers, ultimately we must respect that.

In Lauren's story, she talks about learning something new, and there are instances where trial and error helps rather than hinders. Whether it involves homework, developing friendships or something else, learning, in all ways, is enriched through error. Learning from mistakes is part of how we challenge ourselves to do things differently. It motivates us to try new, innovative approaches to problem-solving. Over a lifetime, learning from mistakes helps develop wisdom and good judgement.

An article in the *Scientific American* magazine makes the case for more challenging tests that force kids to make errors. Historically, educators have created conditions for learning that don't encourage errors. And parents have followed suit. For example, if we drill children over and over again with the same maths problem, they will eventually remember the answer. And if they're lucky, they will remember the answer on a standardised test.

Contrary to popular belief, when a person makes a mistake while learning, it *improves* their memory for the right information. According to a study published in the journal *Memory*, "mistakes that are a 'near miss' can help a person learn the information better than if no errors were made at all." Dr Nicole Anderson, senior author of the paper and senior scientist at Baycrest Rotman Research Institute, says, "These types of errors can serve as stepping stones to remembering the right answer. But if the error made is a wild guess and out in left field, then a person does not learn the correct information as easily."

It's All About the Effort

Dr Carol Dweck, whom we have mentioned in previous chapters, is a psychologist and professor at California's Stanford University. She studies the importance of challenging children to learn from mistakes. Her research shows that praising children for their intelligence can actually make them less likely to persist in the face of challenge.

She and her colleagues followed hundreds of fifth-grade children (aged 10–11) in New York City schools. When the fifth-graders were challenged with an extremely difficult test designed for eighth-graders, a surprising result occurred. The students who had been praised for their effort worked very hard, even though they made a lot of mistakes. The kids praised for being smart became discouraged and saw their mistakes as a sign of failure. Intelligence testing for the kids praised for their effort increased by 30 per cent while the kids praised for their intelligence dropped by 20 per cent.

Giving meaningful and specific praise motivates children to learn from mistakes. Praise should focus on developing their character strengths and helping them understand their abilities. It's an opportunity to develop a child's resilience, a topic we will discuss in greater detail in chapter 4.

In thinking about how myself and my husband praise our children, I wondered about the role fathers play in the conversations around making mistakes. I've found that fathers often affect the lives of their young adult daughters in intriguing and occasionally surprising ways. I wondered about how our girls' relationships with their fathers might affect academic performance, and as a consequence, career success.

I had been reading an article by Linda Nielsen, who is a professor of educational and adolescent psychology at Wake Forest University in North Carolina. Linda is the author of *Father-Daughter Relationships: Contemporary Research & Issues* and *Between Fathers & Daughters: Enriching and Rebuilding Your Adult Relationship*. Nielson says that during a girl's teenage years, a daughter needs her father as much as ever. She says that a girl whose father has been actively engaged, throughout her childhood, in promoting her academic or athletic achievements and encouraging her self-reliance and assertiveness, is more likely to graduate from college and have a higher paying, traditionally "male" job.

She goes on to say that she notices how many college and professional female athletes often credit their fathers for helping them to become tenacious, self-disciplined, ambitious and successful. So although it is perhaps more common to hear that boys need their fathers to help develop their adventurous side, we shouldn't dismiss the fact that girls need their fathers to develop their adventurous side, too.

I thought the relationship between father and daughter (where applicable in your family unit) is an interesting subject for us to explore further. I already knew in advance who I wanted to contribute to this chapter and he, in return, particularly wanted to get involved.

I met entrepreneur and business coach David McQueen back in 2017, when we spoke to a large audience of students at a football club conference centre. David's keynote was fun, uplifting, heartfelt, energic and – most of all – honest. Unbelievably, I then had to follow his keynote with my own, which made me feel somewhat unworthy! However, contrary to that, David told me he loved my keynote and that, even to this day, he has my top three takeaways written on the notes on his iPhone. I suppose the point I'm making here is that my keynote and David's keynote were completely different. Probably neither was perfect – and I'm always striving to be better – but what was important that day was what was said.

Since then, I have stayed in touch with David and I'm so pleased I asked him to contribute to my book. A father of two daughters himself, David is an international speaker, executive coach and board advisor. His experience spans almost thirty years of speaking to corporate, public and third-sector audiences, so he has oodles of experience delivering keynotes to large auditoriums. He has hosted conferences and awards in the tech and startup spaces across the world, including Sir Richard Branson's VOOM, Shell LiveWIRE, Startups

Awards, SFEDI and Social Enterprise. More recently, David founded Legacy71, a tech incubator for Black founders. His vision is for his company to be part of a wider narrative, empowering Black techies to take their futures into their own hands.

———

Celebrating What Makes Us Unique
by David McQueen

When it came to exams, I always felt very pressured as a teen. My parents are from the Caribbean, having come to the UK in the late 1960s. Their integration into the UK played a huge part in how they expected us to navigate the education system. For them, they viewed our education as the only way for us to get any kind of advantage in the way of work. What that meant for my siblings and me was a large focus on being able to achieve and go far. Our educational achievements were therefore put first and foremost, before anything else.

Despite my academic successes, my default was always creative. I liked the arts, I liked music and sports, but those were played down by my parents as something you could do secondarily, after being top of the class in English, maths and science. Those were the kind of demands placed on us. As a teen, I truly lacked that balance so important to education – the balance between hard work and creativity.

In raising my own daughters, I really wanted to make sure that despite my high expectations academically, I allowed them creativity in their learning – to see the world in its wider contexts.

Primarily, I make sure my daughters have access to that rounded education. Rather than just reading the textbooks and taking exams, I want them to have an experience of their knowledge applied in the wider world. If we go out for the day, they plan our train journey; if we go to places of historical interest, it's for them to go and look up and find out what the details are. I encourage them to use their education in ways I never did. In no way did I ever resent my parents for how I was raised; they were doing the best for us and I'm really grateful for the kind of education that they gave me. However, when it comes to raising girls now, I wanted to make sure my daughters saw education beyond schooling – that they saw it as a means of understanding their place in the wider world, being able to be innovative and creative and being able to understand other people as well as maths.

When it came to exam stress, my experience as an educator working with hundreds of other students in this situation allowed me to help my own daughters effectively. I was able to give them tips and guidance on how to manage their stress by themselves. They both wanted to achieve for themselves as well as for us, so they were under pressure. As a parent, it can be hard to watch your children stress over that history exam or their English presentation, and my personal advice would be to simply give them a getaway space if they need one. There were times when I would just close my girls' books and take them for a drive, or a walk – just take them away from those hours of study.

Our girls often need that permission to take a break and permission to say, "Yes, I have worked hard, but it's also important to play hard so I don't get overwhelmed by the stress." Avoid watching your child while they sit and overthink about the actual tests and the perfect answers. Instead, engage them in practical conversations about their work, and encourage them to teach you something new! Provide them with that space to find their answers without tests and grades.

With one daughter attending a single-sex school, and the other having a mixed education, I saw them navigate very different challenges. For one, navigating that space as a young woman in a mixed school presented pressures. For the other, being a high-achiever often left her feeling bad – she loved to do things well. As a parent to both, I encouraged them to follow their interests. Often it was very easy for them to compare themselves to each other. Teenage girls find it very hard not to compare, but I always encouraged my girls to be themselves.

A key issue arose in how they navigated the space of being one of the few Black girls in their year groups. Often, my daughters would have to educate and confront peers who weren't exposed to people from different racial backgrounds. The language some of their peers used and the assumptions they made about other people who were Black or from a different background were challenging. Having to navigate that was an interesting part of the conversations we had.

Their identity, how they dealt with conflict and how they were able to educate people when they felt they may be going slightly wrong was something my girls dealt with throughout their school years. It was important to me to help them understand that, as they navigate through this world, there will be so many different factors – their gender, their race, their origin, their class – that may get in their way. There are always issues around gender, class, ethnicity and so on. For me, it is just as important to help teens understand how to navigate these issues, as it is for them to succeed in exams.

A key lesson for children is to never be afraid of individuals who have a different point of view to you. Having that conversation will show your daughter that they can deal with these things in life in their own way, by making their own choices and having their own power. We want them to react in the way they feel best, but also a way that gives them the independence to overcome their challenges themselves.

I told my daughters early on that I was once suspended from school for playfighting in the lunch hall and forcefully (accidentally!) pushing a dinner lady over a table. I was a respectable individual, and very fearful of the consequences, so that experience weighed on me, even at college, because I wanted to make my parents proud. Fast forward a number of years and I was approached by my old head of year, who said, "You remind me of someone: always outspoken, always ready to challenge, but always ready to listen." Since then, we have stayed connected! We met and had lunch, and he told me how amazing it was to see I had that "same fire in my belly" some thirty years later.

As it turns out, this man had fought for me to stay at the school when many others went against him and had wanted me expelled. He didn't want to harm my career or my future; he saw the best in someone he believed in. Sometimes — you may not realise it — there is someone who believes in you, and someone that will see past the troubles you're trying to navigate in growing up. That one person can make a big difference in your life. And *that is why I have been trying to do that in my educational work and as a father – because someone did it for me.*

The key things I want my girls to grow up with are courage, resilience, confidence and, most importantly, kindness. Here's what I want my daughters to know:

- *Being kind is a priority. In navigating this world, the first thing anyone should do is be kind. Show compassion and treat people how they want to be treated. This is integral because it determines how you react to and perceive things. It doesn't mean you're naïve, but shows that you give people the benefit of the doubt until they prove you wrong. Be kind, but protect yourself from being taken advantage of.*
- *Know what your values are. These can be dynamic – they can change as you grow – but set yourself up to know what your boundaries are. Honesty, integrity, accountability, respect. These values shape the kind of work you go into and shape the person you are, the friends you keep, the environment you exist in and so on. What do you want people to know about you?*
- *Agency. Have a sense of self and identity, which, again, can be dynamic. Know who you are and what you stand for, and give yourself the opportunity to speak up when you're asked about your opinions. Never be afraid to celebrate your agency and what makes you up as a young woman, as you navigate the world. Whatever your background, having agency is important. I too often see women too afraid to speak up, but you should never be afraid. Having that agency when you're older, holding your ground and boundaries, is so important.*

Young girls are under a lot of pressure. I think my daughters are good at self-regulating, but it's definitely made harder by social media. You see a lot of imagery and search for validation online. Part of the many conversations we've always had have been around celebrating who they really are, and what makes them amazing, so they don't feel the need to compare. We should all celebrate what draws people to us and what makes us unique, so we don't need to compare ourselves to other people.

Many individuals are successful without the validation of others. There are, though, lots of individuals who go to great lengths to appear a certain way for validation. I think it's more important to be well-read, able to hold a conversation and in possession of social skills, than having looks and digital skills.

I always find it intriguing that my daughters are not embarrassed by me. They're cool to have conversations about me, with a level of respect. I gently remind them that I am not their friend; I'm their dad — but I'm always friendly.

———

When I read the advice from David, what struck me the most were his thoughts on the importance of kindness. Perhaps we underestimate how vital kindness is in how we build and connect every social bond, be that at home, at school or at work. It's an essential component to our evolution. Personally, I have found kindness to be an important trait in a person and it's the quality I remember in people the most. Without the kindness shown to me when I asked David to contribute to this book, his words would not be on these pages at all. David reminds us that we all experience setbacks. Our girls need to find the courage to speak up for themselves and be mindful not to beat themselves up when they make a mistake or fail at something. She will fall and have setbacks; we all do. But these failures can make us stronger, wiser and more real. If your girl failed at something, it means she found the courage to take a chance on something in the first place.

Seven Ways to Teach Your Girl to Accept their Mistakes

Mistakes can help your daughter learn, and, of course, learning to deal with mistakes teaches resilience, but still, mistakes hurt. They can cut into your girl's confidence and make her afraid to try again. Here are some ideas that can help soften the blow and give her the courage and self-belief to have another go.

1. **Encourage her to try new things without being afraid.**

2. **Praise her for her effort and character, rather than the end result.**

3. **Let your daughter know that mistakes are normal and an important part of self-improvement.**

4. **Share examples of your own mistakes, the consequences and how you learnt from them.**

5. **Mentor your daughter on how to apologise when her mistakes have hurt others.**

6. **Teach her to look forward.**

7. **Acknowledge that you don't expect her to get things right every time.**

Conversation 4: "I am rubbish at maths. Even my teacher thinks so!"

School plays an important role in building confidence and resilience, but there is much work to be done. Unfortunately, not everyone has the same opportunity to access the resources that are necessary to build and strengthen their resilience. Many of those in greatest need of resilience have the hardest time accessing the help they need to build protective factors (ways to help them deal more effectively with worrying or stressful events). We build these protective factors by providing a stable home environment or an education, which, in turn, will help them cope with stress.

We know that measuring resilience is complex and there is no magic way to measure it in our children for sure. However, studies show that, from primary school upwards, health, social development and the parenting skills employed at home are contributing factors for resilience building. Other protective factors include achievement at school, successful transitions, good relationships with parents, teachers and peers, and a supportive school environment. In my opinion, children need a feeling of "connectedness".

Girls often say things like, "I'm terrible at this!" and "I can't do it!", which can be so hard for us to hear. No one likes to hear their own children reeling off negative things about themselves. Perhaps we say it too. Often, I'm not even sure that I realise I am doing it.

Sometimes, when girls say these things, they're simply throwaway comments. Perhaps what girls need in those moments is a hug, a chat and some reassurance. They may be harmless. But there is something called "negative self-talk", which experts highlight as harmful, self-critical comments, which can reflect an unhealthy tendency in kids to think the worst of themselves. Negative self-talk can lead to – or be a sign of – something more serious.

We talk a fair amount about perfectionism in this book because it's such a complex topic. I like to compare it with maths, which is such a vast subject, in my view. If you look at maths, you'll find that everyone's level can vary. You could be great in one particular area of maths, yet feel like you can't grasp a different area. No one is perfect at maths – just like no one is perfect in life.

I'm using maths as a metaphor for any subject or pursuit that your daughter finds difficult. I've chosen maths specifically because it is often considered to be a "boy subject", and that feels appropriate. Mathematics surrounds us in everyday life and in so many situations, but even so, many fear it. Many of us have become accustomed to avoiding numerical thinking at all costs. However, it's not only confusing textbooks and subpar teachers that are to blame. We tell ourselves a few untruths, too: maths is inherently hard; only geniuses understand it; we never liked maths in the first place. Often, adults are well-meaning when they tell children about their own maths phobia – after all, won't it make the child feel better if they know others feel the same way?

According to an article I read in *The Telegraph*, the stereotype that maths is a "boy subject" is deep-rooted and enduring. A survey back in 2012, from the campaigning group National Numeracy, showed that, while 71 per cent of men describe themselves as "good or

Mentors and role models for our girls across all different subjects are so important.

excellent" at maths, only 59 per cent of women do. Could a lack of confidence play a part in these results?

I was reading about a woman called Alice Rogers, who read maths at Murray Edwards College in Cambridge (previously known as New Hall College in the 1960s). Alice followed in the footsteps of her mother, who had also been at Cambridge University, doing the same subject, in the 1930s. During Alice's time at Cambridge, she says there was only one female maths lecturer (Dame Mary Cartwright, who, in 1961, became the first ever woman president of the revered London Mathematical Society). Clearly, Dame Mary Cartwright was a lasting role model for Alice, who went on to become professor of mathematics at King's College London.

Mentors and role models for our girls across all different subjects are so important, and it's great to read that Alice Rogers had one who ended up shaping her career in maths. Most of the research shows that women are more worried than men about the prospect of failure. In studies, they often underestimate what they're going to achieve, whereas men are more likely to overestimate. And that fear of failure is perhaps more present in maths – where there are right and wrong answers, and confidence is so important – than, say, in history.

How to Shake off Maths Anxiety

Back in 2012, academics from Oxford and Cambridge Universities said that girls and boys performed roughly the same in independently set maths exams. However, they warned that girls would be pulling ahead if it weren't for increased feelings of apprehension, worry and fear when faced with sums. Another study was published in the *Behavioral and Brain Functions* journal, based on an investigation of 433 British secondary school children. Children aged 11–15 were presented with a maths test and also asked to complete a questionnaire that assessed their physiological, emotional, cognitive and behavioural reactions to the questions. While there was no difference between girls and boys in the test results, the questionnaire found that girls displayed higher levels of mathematical anxiety.

The findings suggest that there is a heightened level of fear that may affect girls' performance in maths exams. Without this level of fear, girls are likely to pull ahead of boys in tests. Nationally, maths is one of the few subjects in which boys perform on par with girls, while girls generally pull ahead in almost all other academic disciplines. In 2019, some 62 per cent of girls achieved five good GCSEs, compared with just 55 per cent of boys.

The National Mathematics Advisory Panel of the US Department of Education has found that anxious students perform lower than their abilities. What's more, there is growing evidence that mathematical anxiety can be passed on, much like a virus, from teachers to students, or possibly from parents to children. As mothers, if we sow the seed in our girls' minds that we are "not good at maths", our girls may, indirectly, pick up the misconception that boys are better at maths than girls.

It's important that, as parents and educators, we nurture our girls' confidence across different subjects, including maths. Where possible, try to spot any early struggles with certain subjects – whether that struggle is intellectual or anxiety-based.

Here are five things you can do at home to help your child with their maths:

- Find some fun maths games you can play together.
- Show your daughter that mistakes are part of the learning process.
- Help her navigate the maths she finds "tricky".
- For visual learners, use coins and other household items to experiment with sums.
- Throw away the idea that you are "bad at maths".

Whatever subject your child feels she's struggling with, encourage her to persevere. If our daughters continue to focus on what they can't do, they continue to see these things as barriers and in turn, they risk running away from achieving the "small wins".

Dealing with Negative Self-Talk

Sometimes, when our girls shout out comments like, "I'm rubbish at maths," it can be hard to know if they're really struggling with self-esteem, or whether they are doing it because they just need some reassurance from us that all is okay.

The important thing I have learnt over the last decade of parenting a daughter is to pay attention to the frequency of these comments. If she's blurting something like this out every day, or every week, then we probably need to address it. If it's once in a while, then perhaps she just needs more of a confidence boost conversation to bring her morale back up to speed. Sometimes spending time with someone who *isn't* a parent, such as a godparent, aunt, uncle or family friend, is a brilliant way to help our girls look at things differently. I'm certain there will be many times when Erin will rock up at one of my friend's houses and knock on the door for a chat. It isn't always a parent or immediate caregiver that they want to open up to.

So, how *do* we spot those times when there really is a problem? Let's be honest, we all speak a bit of negative self-talk at times. Often, as we get older, we just internalise it and try not to vocalise it! But young girls and teenagers don't do that. So here are some signs to look out for that I think should alert you that it may be a problem:

- The negative self-talk is ongoing.
- The child is constantly saying she will fail.
- The ongoing negativity is disrupting her sleep and making her anxious.
- She is making excuses not to go to school.
- It is affecting her close friendship group.

So what can we do to help?

As parents and caregivers, it can sometimes be tempting to ignore our kids when they keep expressing such negative talk, but experts do not recommend brushing it off every time. Whatever their feelings and comments are, we need to listen and validate those concerns to try find out what is going on. Work together and try to steer them away from too much destructive self-talk. We have to give our girls a safe place to talk and convert some of their thoughts back into positive ones. So how can we battle negative self-talk and replace it with optimistic, positive thinking?

I think our next contributor, Mark Martin MBE, might be able to offer some really great advice about how to connect with your daughter and how to motivate her to try to work through those issues that get her down.

Women's rights activist and Nobel Peace Prize laureate, Malala Yousafzai, famously said, "One child, one teacher, one book and one pen can change the world." Well, Mark Martin, also known as the "Urban Teacher", is not your *usual* teacher. He has taught IT (information technology) for more than ten years, and has become an expert in helping teachers and schools use technology to improve teaching and learning. The founder of UKBlackTech, Mark has a passion for education, tech and diversity as well as travelling the world as an inspiring speaker. Mark says that he's always looking at creativity tools that can help make his content and lessons come alive.

When I was at school, I just thought that learning would end as soon as I hit sixteen, but how naïve was I? Now I know very clearly that we are learning every day. Equally, as a parent myself, it has made me consider that I should ask my children more often, "What did you learn today that you didn't know yesterday?"

I asked Mark to share his wisdom on what he sees happening in classrooms and, not just that, but how he wants to support children and young people to enjoy learning, to embrace new opportunities and to learn how to work things through when they go wrong. I love how, in his story, Mark talks about finding "his mountain" – his purpose – and how he hopes other people will find their mountains too.

Live a Life of Learning
by Mark Martin MBE

For the last sixteen years, I've been teaching digital skills to thousands of young people around the country. The work I've done to bridge the gap between education and industry has been well received by the government and the tech and education sectors.

I got into teaching through being a teaching assistant whilst studying for my computer science degree at university. Colleagues at the school were telling me I was great at working with young people, hence I converted my degree over to a teacher's qualification. Now, years later, I've taught thousands of kids digital skills through IT and computer science.

In terms of my personal trajectory at school, I wanted to get into technology. My form tutor (also called Mr Martin) always tried to encourage me to follow my ambitions, and even today I still talk to him as a mentor. He's supported me through my teaching career.

At school, there's always that someone who wants the best for you, but you have to see the best in yourself first, before you listen to it from others. Finding my passion in school was a complex roadmap for me. I knew that whatever I put my energy into, I would always give it my best, whether that was in education, technology or in my personal life. Being positive and shining a light that others can use to see their path is a great legacy to have.

Everything I've done in my life, I've tried my best in. You won't get everything right, but as long as you're making progress and learning from your failures, you are on the right track. I think many young people don't yet know what their passions are, but my advice is to keep curious and try new things.

For me, I discovered my interest in technology at an early age. But not everyone is going to find their passion so early, so if you don't, you keep searching and exploring. Don't be afraid to ask for help and support.

I have worked in a range of schools over the last few years and what I've found is that young people's confidence and outlook on life depends on their social network, support network and confidence network.

Who are the people encouraging and inspiring them?

Students that lack confidence don't necessarily hear enough reinforcement from the adults and peers in their life. Young people's self-esteem is always up and down. There is a lack of consistency in their support networks, and I think this applies to both females and males.

Many young people are encouraged to go down the route of traditional education and traditional career paths. They get lots of support in this, but that comes with a lot of pressure. I think it's more important to ensure that your young person is just equipped for tomorrow, first and foremost. The biggest denominator in terms of confidence comes down to the ecosystem that young people are currently operating in.

In a school environment, the high-stakes testing culture is embedded into the school culture. Preparing students for the outside world isn't just about getting them good grades. It's about developing their soft skills, too, such as public speaking, so they have enough independent skills in their toolbox. When it comes to putting their hand up, all students are different. I think *it depends heavily on how teachers set up the classroom environment. I've heard of some schools that ban putting up your hand. Instead, teachers use randomiser apps to choose which student should answer the question. Teachers try to encourage all young people, in various settings.*

We live in a day and age now where putting yourself out there — whether online or applying for jobs — will often come with criticism. How do we help young people put themselves out there and not be ashamed? Or even just teach them how to process that negative criticism? We need to show young people that getting the answer wrong doesn't make a fool of them. There needs to be more done in teaching young people that it's okay to ask a question or get the answer wrong.

I have always shown my students that failure is only feedback. Failure shouldn't be seen as detrimental or life changing. We need to use failure to see what we can improve upon. We need to realise failure isn't terminal and it is something we can grow from. Part of my teaching routine has always been to incorporate failure in a positive way. I share my own failures with my students, and I share how I have overcome them to be where I am today. Even now, I still fail, but I'm a lifelong learner, and it's only human to meet challenges and overcome them.

Having worked in several all-girls schools before, I think it's so important to keep the communication lines open. Girls need to understand that they can always ask for support at school.

School-age girls, especially when sitting their exams, often put a lot of pressure on themselves and aim to overachieve. This can affect young people both physically and emotionally. We try to encourage inspiring role

"Failure is
only feedback."

MARK MARTIN MBE

models of similar ages to become accessible to girls during stressful periods. Having a role model who is slightly older, perhaps a girl in sixth form or university, has been so successful. Role models of a similar age will speak the same language as a young girl sitting her GCSEs and will be more relatable to young girls than an adult. We need consistency and long-term support for our young females. We need to give motivational talks to girls from a young age and continue that throughout their school journey, as they grow.

Role models don't often realise the impact they will make. Obviously, this impact on a young person can't be measured. What I think could potentially be a game changer would be to track young people in the long-term, to observe the impact of engagement with a role model and observe the potential those young girls reach.

Too often, we see young people saying, "I'm no good at that." As a teacher, I will spot a gifted and talented student and place them on a programme to nurture that skill. As a school, we will actively encourage these young people to take their passions and skills further. We want to celebrate their achievements and talents. The most important thing is that a child's talent is recognised – by themselves and by others.

I've seen many girls come into my computing and IT classes with no confidence and no guidance on what career options are available to them. I've tried to tackle this situation by inviting them to coding clubs and introducing them to guest speakers who might raise their confidence – and their career aspirations.

Exposing young girls to a wider world of opportunities, and empowering them to go away and pursue their *dreams is everything. Providing those networks and showing them there are ways to achieve their goals is so important.*

One of the biggest blockers nowadays is accessing the people in the right industries to inspire young females. As a teacher, it's important that I try to make those connections for students and show them it is possible. I have former students working in cyber security, automobile companies and so on. I like to look back and realise how we have helped those students get where they are.

In order for girls to thrive, we need to show them that anything is possible. In my school, I did this by changing the curriculum to show greater representation and more varied career pathways for women. This helped the girls have a better understanding of how they could potentially see themselves working in the tech world in the future.

———

Mark gives us a teacher's perspective on the conversations we could be having with our children at home. Mark's approach to how he gains the trust of his students makes so much sense. The student buys into the teacher before the student buys into the learning. Mark tells me that teaching is about creating a relationship with a young person and understanding the young person in front of you before they understand that they need to learn something. It's about that human touch, the connection.

When it comes to struggling with a task or a subject, Mark practises what he preaches. He tells me that at one point in his career he was assigned to teach a module of advanced coding, which he said was "out of his depth". Instead of hiding behind his fears or being stressed by it, he decided to join an advanced coding course to help build his skills and knowledge in that area.

Mark's story reminds us that although a commitment to lifelong learning and building skills isn't easy, learning is about growing and developing yourself, your value and who you are. I hope girls can find a teacher or mentor just like Mark – one who can motivate them to broaden their skills every day. As Mark says, "skills are the new currency of the future." By continuing to learn, our girls will have a better chance of getting their dream job, gaining that promotion and contributing their value to a modern world.

Even the brightest of students can still find themselves overwhelmed by the array of subjects in school. If your daughter feels as if she's stuck in a rut with a certain topic or subject matter, there are ways to help her. Start by focusing on the areas where she wants to improve. Watch her work a bit. Perhaps she hasn't found her most effective studying style yet, but if you work on it together, maybe you can help her find a method that works. It may be a case of supporting her to allocate herself extra time on the subject she has identified as "tricky". Focusing on those areas could be the driver she needs to build her confidence in those subjects.

Seven Questions About School to Ask Your Daughter in Seven Days

Discussing problem subjects with your daughter can be touchy. Here are seven conversation starters to help open up the dialogue between you and your daughter about what's going on at school.

1. **What subjects do you think you are good at?**

2. **What subjects would you most like to improve on and why?**

3. **Do you know any older girls or role models who could help you improve in that subject?**

4. **Do test result scores impact how you feel about a subject?**

5. **What does it take to consider yourself "good" at a particular subject?**

6. **How do you judge what you feel you are not good at?**

7. **Which teachers do you most admire and why?**

Conversation 5: "She's really awesome. I wish I could be more like her."

I had never quite grasped how important role models are until I became a parent myself. When I was a teenager, it didn't really cross my mind who may or may not be influencing me, either directly or indirectly. Yet, throughout our lifetime, we will see and meet an array of different people who will become potential role models for us and our girls.

From early childhood, we look up to a variety of role models who can help shape not only the people we become, but also how we behave, at school, outside of school and within relationships. Most of our early role models will be our parents, siblings, teachers, coaches or peers. We may try to copy the behaviour of athletes, celebrities or even characters from books and movies. The list is endless. The important thing is to help our children find positive role models who have the right values.

I recently spoke to Fiona Murden, a chartered psychologist, associate fellow of the British Psychological Society, author and public speaker. I had really enjoyed reading Fiona's book, *Mirror Thinking*, which discusses mirroring and role models. I spoke to Fiona at length about the fascinating way our brains work and why mirroring is more important than we can imagine.

Mirroring can play a crucial role in developing relationships. When we mirror, not only does it stimulate actions, but it can also reflect intentions and feelings. I think about the times I've been in meetings and crossed my arms. Then, all of a sudden, the person sitting opposite crosses her arms. Then I gently touch my hair, and they do the same. As such, mirroring plays a key role in our ability to socialise and empathise with others. I'm definitely no expert in this field, but Fiona definitely is.

Fiona explained to me how the brain works in relation to mirroring: "We have something in our brain that enables us to watch what other people are doing without repeating it as we see it. However, we can rehearse it, both physically and mentally, and learn from it. I mean, how many times have you sat with a friend and when you folded your arms, they did too? It's like looking in a mirror!"

I asked Fiona about how important our actions, as parents, are for our children. She said, "As parents we're only human. We need to own up where we've done wrong, in addition to being a good role model for them. We don't need to be perfect. When it comes to finding role models, we need to look at the values people hold. Why are they doing what they're doing? Are they giving the right message? Are they happy in themselves? I encourage my daughter to find positive role models, and, though this is hard to find, especially on social media, it's important to talk through with our children about what they're looking for in a role model."

I found this fascinating and there were so many more questions I wanted to ask her. There was a section in Fiona's book that had caught my eye. In fact, I had even underlined it with my highlighter. It was about a US study, which said that by the age of eleven, children spend approximately 33 per cent of their spare time with their siblings. I wondered what influence siblings had on our girls and I asked Fiona if we learn from mirroring siblings.

"It's interesting," she replied, "because we never presume that we're learning from simply spending time with siblings, but we're hugely influenced by them! Adult females tend to have their first child at roughly the same time as their sisters. The mirroring behaviours we learn in childhood from our siblings will carry on throughout life. In a Chinese study, psychologists found that single children have less empathy than children with siblings, and this could well be due to the absence of mirroring in childhood."

I would assume my daughter, Erin, is an influence on her brothers, Seth and Nico. In return, I hope that both Seth and Nico will be positive role models for Erin – even if they don't even realise they are. Indeed, research shows that although older siblings will act as role models for their younger siblings, the relationship can work both ways. This fits with my own experience of watching my children play and learn together.

As a final question, I asked Fiona how we can try to raise kind, empathetic children who have the confidence to be their best selves. She replied, "I think we must keep reminding them. Our children's awareness comes partly from themselves, but partly from us. We must keep reminding our children to be active, get out there and socialise with positive people. Teens are more prosocial (they display behaviours that benefit others, including sharing, donating, co-operating and volunteering) when surrounded by others who are prosocial! The key thing is, we are all human and it's okay to get it wrong. That's what learning is all about."

I realised at that point that Fiona and I had touched on something so important. The simple art of human connection. Fiona had reminded me that we have to focus on simple human connections and allow ourselves to nurture our time with others, and with ourselves. I felt quite emotional speaking to Fiona about this, mostly because it made me recognise how Erin is a huge influence and role model for me – meaning that my eleven-year-old daughter can be just as much of an influence on me as any other human being. If it were not for Erin, her kindness and ambitious nature to be her best self, I don't think this book would ever have come to life. She'd been my role model all along, but I'd barely realised it until that moment.

Role models are so important, and when it came to writing this section, I had already considered a couple of individuals who are brilliant at lifting up other women as well as helping our younger generations find their voice.

Anna Jones is a British entrepreneur and former CEO of magazine giant Hearst, which publishes many magazines in the UK, including *Red*, *ELLE*, *Harper's Bazaar* and *Cosmopolitan*. Since stepping down from this role in 2017, Anna, never afraid to put her hand up and try something new, dived straight in to start a business from scratch after coming up with an idea on a small scrap of paper.

Anna is the co-founder of AllBright, an organisation with a network of angel investors, a crowdfunding platform and an academy, which aims to support female-led startups and encourage women to invest.

AllBright, which Anna co-founded with Debbie Wosskow, is a growing community that connects entrepreneurial, inspiring women from across the globe. I myself am a proud founding member of AllBright and, using my own voice, I welcome and encourage other women to join as members.

AllBright's very name was inspired by the famous Madeleine Albright quote, "There's a special place in hell for women who don't help other women."

I felt that including Anna's advice in this chapter would be extremely valuable because she is someone who is all about giving young women the ability to share their voice. She believes that there is no stopping what we can do.

———

There's Nothing a Girl Can't Do
by Anna Jones

I was born in Harrogate and grew up in rural Yorkshire. We lived in the middle of nowhere! I am the eldest of four girls and I was brought up by my Danish mother, who had a very Scandinavian take on equality (men and women are equal!) and my father, who, with four daughters, always thought of himself as feminist.

My parents believed there was nothing a girl couldn't do, and therefore I was brought up to believe there was nothing I couldn't do. Where I lived, we weren't that connected with the world, and my parents were not all that involved in what we did. They said, "As long as you do your best and as long as you're working hard, that's fine."

"What's the worst that can happen?" was an ongoing piece of advice from my parents.

As a young girl in a small village school, it wasn't hard to stand out. Maybe I was precocious, but I believed there was nothing I couldn't do. I moved schools five times as a child, which led me to learn to navigate new environments. This really helped me build up my resilience from a young age and has definitely shaped who I am.

As a young girl, I was crazy about magazines. Coming into my teenage years, magazines were a small window into a really glamorous world, far from home, and that was exciting. I did a business degree and wrote my dissertation on the media and magazines. I wanted to work in marketing and developed some background by working various jobs when I first graduated. And then I found my dream job. I didn't have the required skills, but I applied and got an interview. I was so passionate that, despite my lack of skills, I got the job! My passion was so important, and I was trained and mentored along the way. Over the following years, the magazine industry became more challenging, but hard work and passion goes a long way. Being that person who says, "I'll do it!" has built my career.

After working on a big launch at my magazine, a smaller publishing company invited me for a cup of tea. I met the chairman, who persuaded me to join him as his marketing director. It was a huge opportunity. I just thought, "I'll go for it," and entered one of the biggest crossroads of my career.

My boss became a sponsor for me, and he truly pushed me forward. He had a sense for when I was getting itchy feet and, at those times, would give me another role or a different part of the business to run. He was very direct and, to many, seemed curt and scary, but although he was tough, he always believed in me. Someone like that can have a huge impact on a young woman's life. Being an active sponsor for someone can make a very big difference to them.

When the company merged with another, at his recommendation I became COO and, a couple of years later, CEO, which was a mammoth challenge to take on. It was one of my steepest learning curves. I was the first female CEO in the company's 100-year history.

Being the only woman sitting around the boardroom table became a common thing, and I was often asked both how and why I smashed that glass ceiling. But with a team made up of 77 per cent women, it was frustrating to see there were hardly any around the boardroom table. I made changes to that "tradition" by hiring and promoting women into senior leadership roles and, as one of my first moves as CEO, introduced an "Empowering Women" project across all magazines. I brought all the magazine editors – traditionally competitors – together to stand up for women, turning something holding us back into something much more powerful that would take us forward.

My biggest career sponsor was a man, and many other successful women have a similar story. Men so often have access to an extended and connected network that can make opportunities reality, and we need to ensure they are on the journey to equality with us as supporters and enablers.

The next moment of serendipity in my life was meeting my AllBright co-founder, Debbie Wosskow. We both had a shared passion-point for empowering women, and our conversations were often spent musing, "Where are all the women?" Even beyond the boardroom level, the statistics showed there was a major lack of female representation in business. I felt women wanted to move into the driving seat of their careers, and this is something Debbie felt too.

We began thinking about what was missing for women. More often than not it was a network. We wanted a network for women – a space where they could come together and learn together. Women are much better at communicating, but often don't extend that communication beyond those they already know. If we could create a community of women that could inspire each other, connect and share with each other, it would be extremely powerful. We wanted a space where women could pitch their ideas and share their experiences.

A few years down the line, it's been really heartening to see the connections people are making through AllBright. We've seen role models growing, women inspiring, hiring, promoting and supporting other women – and a whole lot of sisterhood.

My daughter, aged eleven, has already told me she wants to be an entrepreneur. She's always coming up with business ideas, and I want that to be normal for her. I think even at her age, being a girl is tough. I encourage her to believe in herself and try to involve her as much as possible in my career. I try to surround her with incredible role models because being surrounded by a supportive network is so important.

I always tell my children there are two things to do:

- *Work hard and try your best.*
- *Be kind.*

"We have to show that there is 'nothing a girl can't do', because that's exactly what my parents taught me."

ANNA JONES

I think instilling resilience in our daughters is a natural pathway to increase confidence. Teenagers suffer with self-esteem, which is only further magnified with the rise of social media. Building resilience, and teaching girls to pick themselves up again when things go wrong, is how they learn to believe in who they are. As a parent, talk about your own failures as well as what you succeed in. It's important to show them when you are picking yourself up again, and really congratulate them when they do the same.

In today's world, we tend to measure ourselves against others all the time. Teach your children to understand the bigger picture, and use these comparisons as helpful resources for their own journey. There is always going to be someone better than you — so we must teach them to aspire, without feeling deflated. If your child is truly amazing, but someone else is Olympic standard, don't compare — but allow her to be encouraged. Allow that comparison to push her further in bettering herself. Use others' achievements as fuel for your own. It's not easy, but it is important.

To be a leader you need to be decisive, determined and clear in your mission, but you also need to have these important qualities: being positive, kind, open and vulnerable. Trying to help our children navigate that stuff is very important but really challenging. The only way I see through it, is to keep showing them different role models and help keep communication really open. We have to show that there is "nothing a girl can't do", because that's exactly what my parents taught me.

There are many things we can learn from successful female entrepreneurs like Anna. Most of all, I love that it was her parents who instilled in her from a young age that there was "nothing a girl can't do", a motto that has stayed with her for life. Goodness, if only we told our girls this more often!

And when it comes to sponsors, Anna's sponsor was hugely impactful on her early career. I think it's brilliant that it was Anna's boss who was willing her to keep aiming higher. It reminds us that you don't have to know it all to take on a big role, but you have to have that self-belief to go for it in the first place. This reinforces the significance again of positive role models and mentors in our girls' lives, because they're the ones who can guide our girls when they're feeling lost.

Many of us can relate to the worry that our girls will compare themselves to others. I love Anna's suggestion to use these comparisons as fuel for your own achievements. It is so powerful to be able to turn a potentially negative comparison into something useful, even advantageous. We should learn from *every* person – positive role models and negative ones – and turn something that could be harmful into a learning experience.

Just like Anna's sponsor, who believed in her and supported her career progress, and just like the objectives of AllBright, which are to empower and grow women in business, Anna truly embodies the message she has just shared: that if we find someone who champions us, we can eventually take that learning and learn how to champion ourselves.

When we find women of influence, we need to tap into that resource to show girls that they deserve to aim high. The collection of stories we tell our girls can encourage them to strive for great things. Not every girl may want to be a CEO, prime minister or president, but if they do, why not?

The Girls' Network is a great example of how to use the power of role models. A UK charitable organisation, it works hard to positively impact teenage girls' lives by pairing them with professional women who can help them achieve their potential. Each girl receives a mentor, work experience, workshops, networking events and a lifelong membership to their ambassador network, because as the saying goes, "You can't be what you can't see."

June Angelides MBE is an entrepreneur, investor, mentor and advisor to startups. Using her extensive knowledge and experience, she supports women of colour to get the business investment they deserve. Her podcast series, called *Believe it, Achieve it*, is a great example of the work she's doing to support more female founders and founders of colour.

In 2020, June received an MBE for founding the coding school, Mums in Technology, an immersive learning experience that encourages new mothers to learn how to code. Named the fifteenth most influential woman in tech by *Computer Weekly,* and one of the top ten most influential BAME tech leaders in the UK, June is one to watch. I thought she would be the perfect person to talk about the importance of role models.

———

Inspiration Comes from Having Different Role Models
by June Angelides MBE

As a teen, I was really shy. I had all these big ideas but would never put my hand up. I always wanted to join in with the confident girls on stage, but I didn't. Knowing my family background of actors and entertainers, one would just assume confidence ran in my blood, and, though for me the desire was there, I had a big lack of confidence. I let my fear hold me back, and it was when I looked back on these missed opportunities that I decided to get on with it and pluck up the courage to be me. Don't worry about what people think. I had a fear of judgement and failure. I wish I had the mindset earlier that it was okay to try things and not be good at it. I wish someone had given me permission to fail.

Furthering my education, I studied economics at UCL, where my confidence was still lacking. Looking back now, I had this "good girl syndrome" – wanting to do everything right. And I did; I smashed my A-levels. But I missed out on all the adventure education brings with it. My fear of judgement and networking held me back from joining societies – you need confidence to approach new people in that social environment. I wish I had done more of that. I could have made more out of that opportunity. Now, I feel like I'm making up for lost time, grabbing opportunities and learning to say yes more. The power of yes. We have to be willing to try, experience new things, and not worry too much.

In the six weeks following my C-section, I had a lot of thinking time, especially about what I wanted my return to work to look like. I went back and instantly felt out of place; I couldn't remember my job since I'd immersed myself in all things baby. By baby number two, I was conscious not to repeat this experience and I wanted to keep my brain active. Initially, I considered taking courses online but found nothing that fit. That's when I started thinking about building an app for people like me, and hence I had to learn the technology.

I set out on my journey and wanted to bring others along with me. I wanted to meet people with a similar mindset to me. Mums in Technology allowed me to discover part of myself I had never tapped into. I wanted to find my tribe, who would give me confidence. I realised I wasn't alone, and I was motivated to want new things.

Going back to what made me feel nervous as a teen, it was that fear of judgement. It's important we give girls that safe space where they can express themselves. Constantly remind them, "Do not be afraid, this is a safe space." It's important for them to feel this. Constantly remind them, "It's okay to express yourself." Listen to them and their cues.

My daughters love expressing themselves through drama, but only in small, safe environments. This is where they gain their confidence. Find where your own daughter's outlet is. Explore, and allow her to feel like a master of one small thing — that confidence will transfer.

Women supporting women — there's nothing more beautiful. People need to be aware that helping another woman rise doesn't diminish you. We all do better if we all push each other up. Someone helped me get where I am and explore my ideas, guiding me and believing in me. Having a stranger believe in me really showed me the huge power of mentoring I hadn't known before. That one person believing in you makes all the difference, and now, if I can have a conversation with someone and have the same impact on them – I am satisfied. Though life is hardly an easy ride for anyone, it's important not to let negative experiences distort our view of how we want to be. Don't let those who take advantage of you get in the way of you helping someone else.

All women look different, but my advice is to embrace everybody since we are all one. Seeing powerful, successful women from all kinds of backgrounds, from all age groups, making a difference, is amazing to see. Some of the busiest women make sure they find the time to help others – because they realise the importance of role modelling. You don't go out choosing to have the label of a role model, but as it turns out, things you do can inspire others, and that's why it's important to share your story. Role models provide inspiration. You can be a role model without knowing it, an accidental role model.

It's important to find role models your teen can connect and relate to. Thinking back to how I felt as a teen, I was confused about what direction I wanted my life to go in. I found that having people come into school and having that chance to meet different types of people was so important. Teens need to meet people from all backgrounds to keep all the options open.

Help your daughter be open-minded because how else can she form a sense of the world? Now, we need to give girls the opportunity to make up their own minds, by providing them with enough information from as many different people as possible.

As a parent, you may often be your child's first role model — followed closely by family friends, teachers, coaches — and there's a great importance in having different types of role models. Resilience is something I found in my Gran, who made every situation work for her, made sacrifices and put others first. Looking at her, she was so inspiring, one of my first role models. But then I also found a different role model in my aunt, who always taught me to "never hold a grudge", and that's something I've also always remembered. I may be too kind, but there's nothing worse than having a grudge holding you down. That sort of advice, heard young from someone you love, ends up being so helpful in navigating through life.

How can we help girls grow their passions?

I'm constantly thinking, "What will my daughter decide she wants to do? How do I steer her in the right direction?" I must remember it's up to her. I must give her the opportunity to try new things and meet many different people. Our daughters need to hear different conversations and realise the opportunities of the world. As parents, we must keep her curious, keep her learning and keep her exploring different sides of herself. Keep listening to her cues. It will be up to her — and that might be hard, but all you want is for your daughter to be happy. A well-rounded, happy and confident girl.

For me, the most important qualities to teach my girls are kindness, happiness, confidence and being fearless leaders. We want girls who are willing to explore new things, and who realise the power of giving back.

"Teach them compassion and teach them not to be afraid to be truly themselves."

JUNE ANGELIDES MBE

Continue the cycle of kindness. We want kind, strong leaders. Kindness doesn't make you weak. We need our girls to have the belief that they can make a decision without waiting for permission.

Teach your girls empathy because empathy is so important in a strong leader. Teach them compassion and teach them not to be afraid to be truly themselves. That's when the power comes out and you feel you can do anything. We are all human, and hence we are all equal – that's where the power of authenticity comes in. We must teach our girls that not everyone has to like them, and that's okay. We must tell them to do their best then to move past even that, and carry on doing the right thing for themselves.

———

June brings clarity to an important point that, as parents and caregivers, what our girls decide to do, will – and should – be their choice. When it comes to role models, there are so many women of influence and intellect in the world, that together we can support our girls to relish the opportunities that life will present them. June shows herself to be a true ambassador for women and girls with her aim to motivate all of us to dream big without fear.

June said she was shy at school and would never put her hand up, but by slowly finding her confidence, her levels of self-belief started to soar.

Collectively, I believe that Anna, June and myself would all like to see more role models brought into schools. Reach out to your school, college or university to ask what they are doing to show more inspiring role models to our girls. In my opinion, in many cases, it should not be a matter of cost. So many smart, successful, kind, compassionate women are willing to volunteer an hour of their time to help a generation of thinkers and creators. Are parents being asked to come in and share their stories with the class?

Together, we can seek out role models in everyday life who will help us bring out the best in our girls. Do you have a good story to tell that would make you a good role model?

Seven Ways to Help Girls Find Great Role Models

Role models have a huge impact on girls and women because when girls see women rising, it spurs on their own ambitions to rise as well.

1. **Introduce them to someone who can teach them about their successes and failures.**

2. **Find someone who is different to them.**

3. **Find someone who can teach them important values, such as the power of kindness and gratitude.**

4. **Find someone who can help them grow their confidence and find their passions.**

5. **Help them find someone who is brilliant at reflecting on experiences.**

6. **Introduce them to someone who can help them focus on their individual strengths.**

7. **Find someone who helps them understand their voice and how to use it, and who can teach them to raise their hand!**

Conversation 6: "Why would she say that? I thought she was my friend."

Last year, I went into my daughter's bedroom and perched myself on her bed for a chat, like I often do. She seemed quieter than normal that evening and I asked her if everything was okay. She didn't say much in reply, so I gently enquired again. "Actually, Mum," she replied, "there is something I wanted to talk to you about." And with that, she went on to tell me that one of the girls at school was being mean to her. I asked her to tell me what had happened. "Well…" she said, "she was just being really unkind. Telling me that I shouldn't be in the A-team at netball as I have a loopy shoulder pass. She said she was going to take my place in the team and that I'll be moved down to a lower squad." *Okay*, I thought to myself. *That doesn't sound like something a friend should say.* "But that's not all, Mum," she continued. "She went on to say that I played for a rubbish rugby team and that I was too weak to play rugby anyway. She told me I wasn't strong."

As a parent, your immediate reaction is to protect and I could feel the anger building inside me, not that I wanted to show that to Erin. I tried really hard to suppress how I was feeling. Everything felt quiet for a moment and I could see that Erin was upset by how she'd been treated by her friend. I wondered how Erin had responded to that girl. There are so many ways you can respond or react when someone is being unkind to you. You can run away, you can cry, you can shout back or you can do nothing but feel hurt. In this moment, I got my very first experience as a mother of how it feels for your daughter to be put down by a friend.

After a minute or so, I asked Erin how she'd replied when this "friend" said those unkind words to her. With that, Erin turned to me, confidently, and said, "I looked her in the eyes and told her that being strong comes from the inside." And the other girl had turned away and walked off. Erin's positive response had given the girl an answer she wasn't expecting and with that, there was no comeback. How can you challenge such a positive answer like that?

Even to this day, that remains one of my proudest moments with Erin. I will never forget sitting on her bed with her, hearing about how she had dealt with a difficult situation all by herself. I wish that when I was her age, I'd had the confidence to give such a smart answer in return.

When I considered the words that the girl used when speaking so unkindly to Erin, I ended up thinking more about that girl than I did about Erin. This is because, in my experience, during adolescence a mean girl often acts out of jealousy or insecurity. Therefore, what she was criticising about Erin was actually nothing to do with Erin. For some reason, projecting her own behaviour onto someone else made her feel good.

Fortunately, there are ways to tackle this type of behaviour. We need to spread the message of how we should be treating each other. We should encourage girls and women to lift one another up rather than tearing one another down.

As parents, we often try to encourage our girls to support their friends, to raise them up and not to see each other as competition all the time. So why are girls prone to see one another as competition? And how can parents encourage them to build empowering friendships that lift each other up instead?

Part of the reason girls are prone to compete is that they worry about losing out on opportunities, which in turn, could lead them to believe that their own success will be limited. A recent survey by Plan International USA showed that 30 per cent of teenage girls feel they have fewer opportunities at school than boys do, particularly when it comes to sports and leadership. This means that if a girl loses one chance to another girl, she might conclude that she'll never get another one. Business leader and professional basketball pioneer Donna Orender says, "Unfortunately, it's been communicated to us over the years that there are fewer spots for women – a limited inventory."

So what can we do to help our girls with this?

An important first step is to help your daughter grow her self-confidence. We know from many studies that confidence tends to drop significantly in girls as they reach the tween years, so it's up to us to help them build it back up again. Show your daughters positive images of confident girls and women standing with strength, which helps reinforce confidence messages. Maybe you've heard of or seen the *Fearless Girl* sculpture in New York? It is a great example of a confident girl. She stands strong with her feet apart, her hands on her hips, boldly staring down Wall Street. This is what we need to show our girls.

It's also important that parents teach their kids to value personal mastery and improvement more than how their performance compares to others. For example, if she's a runner, instead of asking herself if she ran further or faster than others, she should be asking herself if she ran further or faster than she did yesterday.

Help her focus on achieving her personal best. It's possible to be competitive without thriving on doing better than someone else. Moreover, encouraging girls to join a team – not necessarily just a sports team, but any group with a shared goal – helps them learn how to invest in one another's success and build each other up. I think it's fair to say that not many of us achieve greatness in isolation.

Of course, competition *can* be beneficial to girls. It can help them build confidence and assertiveness, as long as they know there's a respectful way to do it. We've been so militant about getting girls to be nice, they don't even know there's such a thing as healthy competition. Encourage girls to do their best in competitive situations, but emphasise the importance of good sportsmanship and empathy throughout.

Another way that girls can help lift one another up is by using the power of social media for good. While surveys have found that many girls believe society most values their physical appearance, we can encourage girls to change this dynamic by celebrating one another's substantive achievements on social media.

Positive relationships and role models are everywhere. But when you go looking online to find a role model for your own daughter, just remember *you* are one. Take her by the hand, build her confidence and show her how to achieve her personal best, while still celebrating the success of her friends.

What Does a Good Friend Look Like?

We can't choose our daughter's friends, but we can teach them how to choose the right friends. Before we start getting into the nitty gritty of mean girls and toxic friendships, we should first look at how friendships are formed and what good friendships look like. As adults, we have already learnt that good, long-lasting friendships are important for our mental wellbeing. Perhaps we've started to take some of those friendships for granted? For some of us, these friendships may have spanned thirty or so years. Isn't that incredible? But what is it that makes a good friendship stick?

Children start building meaningful friendships around the age of four or five. These relationships can be with classmates, neighbourhood kids, cousins or the children of a parent's friends. As parents, we want to ensure our children know how to choose the *right* friends.

The interesting thing is that friendships are often nurtured through parent involvement, whether it's because we encourage them to play with children of our own friends, or because we try to introduce them to new friends we think will be a good fit for their personality. For example, many of us parents will try to match our children with other children who have similar, shared interests, and it is solely on that basis that we hope they will build lasting friendships.

Another element to consider here, is that our children may copy the friendship relationships we have with our own friends, so how we show what a good friendship look like is important. Through our own friendships, we demonstrate to our children how we communicate with others, how we share, how we encourage and lift someone else up when they're feeling sad. I hadn't thought too much about the fact that my children probably watch my own friendships from a distance, but now I find it fascinating to think about how much they see and how much they mimic what we do with our friends. When we're in front of our closest friends, we're at our most happy and relaxed. Kids are always watching, and this is another prime example of the early guidance they lean on you for.

Friends offer support to each other when they are sad, upset, hurt, scared, happy and excited. They are also there to celebrate each other's accomplishments. A good friend will offer support, encouragement and kindness because their friend means a lot to them. When your daughter asks you what a good friend looks like, you can tell her all these things. We call these people "cheerleaders".

A good friend is also an inclusive friend. One who doesn't exclude others or make them feel unwanted. A good friend will be happy for you when you get elected to school council or sports captain and doesn't unleash the green monster of *jealousy*. She'll put her arm around you and genuinely show she's excited and happy for you. If your daughter understands this from observing your friendships, she will remember to do the same when her friend gets elected next time around.

According to a report about friendships that I read in *Psychology Today*, 7–12-year-olds are able to consider a friend's perspective in addition to their own, but not at the same time. So, this means that they understand turn-taking, but they have difficulty stepping back to look at the bigger picture, which would allow them to see patterns of interaction in their relationships.

It's interesting to see that, at this stage in their childhood development, children are very concerned about fairness and reciprocity. So, if they do something nice for a friend, they expect that friend to do something nice for them at the next opportunity. If this doesn't happen, the friendship is likely to become fractured, and I've seen examples of this with my own daughter.

I love to hear from Erin about how she remembered to save a seat on the minibus for a friend when they were going to a netball match. But then, will she be thinking about who will do that for her next time they take the minibus? Right now, Erin believes that friendships are completely symmetrical two-way relationships. Just like the concept of karma, where we do something nice because we hope something nice will come back to us.

From the age of twelve, our girls start to really value the emotional closeness they have with their friends. They start to gain more perspective of what friendship means and, at this more complex stage, find it easier to appreciate differences between themselves and their friends. As their friendships naturally grow and mature, the importance of trust and support moves into the spotlight, replacing the reliance on immediate and direct reciprocity.

Help Your Girl Navigate Friendship Problems

How would your daughter feel if someone started to mock her at school for something she liked? Playing out those scenarios at home in advance will help your daughter learn how to manage that situation if and when it happens.

What if your daughter loves sewing club at school and her friend says it's lame? How will she respond to that?

What's your daughter going to say to the person who says she is too weak to play rugby?

What do you tell your daughter to say when there's a party, but she hasn't been invited?

These things happen every day and we need to teach our daughters how to deal with them. Role play is such an effective learning tool for this kind of thing. Showing her that you understand will encourage her to confide in you more.

Sit down with your daughter, or chat in the car about how you can explore options together for managing awkward or uncomfortable situations like these. Even if these scenarios aren't happening right now, it's good to understand how your daughter would approach them, both inside and outside of the classroom. Teach her about potential options by asking, "What could you do to stop someone being unkind with their words, without harming anyone in return?" or, "What would you do if you saw one of your friends being picked on?"

I wish there was more we could do to stop the negativity, but there is no one-size-fits-all approach to this. However, I believe it's important for our girls to stand up for themselves when they feel comfortable doing so. Similarly, friends can look out for each other. If they see the other being picked on, they can immediately join forces, tell the offender to stop and walk off together. If they see that the situation is physically dangerous or threatening, they can go find the closest caring adult and enlist their support. Giving your daughter a safe space where she can talk to an adult is really crucial. I dread the day my daughter will say, "Mum, can I have a private chat with you, please?" – and for that conversation to be about how she's being picked on at school. But I would be proud of her for telling me. I know many girls and young women keep things like that a well-guarded secret through fear of making the situation worse. But it's important that they talk to someone they trust.

From chatting to friends about how we want to raise our children, the most common response is that we want to raise kind, well-mannered, happy, well-rounded children. It sounds so simple, doesn't it? But we all know raising children is hard. Kindness and good manners are not something that should be taken for granted. After we left a café with our children at the weekend, I asked the children to make sure they said thank you to the waitress as we left. It hit me that some of the traditional manners seem to be dying out or are being forgotten. I had to prompt my children to say thank you in the hope that next time they might remember without the nudge from Mum. How will we teach them to remember to open the door for people, respect their elders or help their friends without being asked? Perhaps some of these basic social skills help to frame our friendships?

On another occasion, when we came out of a shop one day, my son noticed that the man in front of us had dropped a ten-pound note. My son immediately picked it up and said, "Excuse me. You dropped some money," and handed it back to him. I was beaming with pride that our son had done this unprompted. I can only imagine how tempted he might have been to have kept the money, but life is about trying to do the right thing, whatever that right thing is at the time.

I don't want to take small acts of kindness like this for granted because I think some of these basic acts will help nurture our children's relationships with others, especially within friendship groups. So, I ask you this: How can our children move forward in life, as decent human beings, if we don't encourage these simple acts? Teach your kids these general manners so they don't become long-lost in the future. The smallest acts of kindness can change someone's day, and someone's perspective.

Bullying Behaviour

Child clinical and school psychologist Dr Paulo Pires, from Milton, Canada, says, "From 9–11 – what we call middle childhood – kids start to gain awareness of similarities and differences within peer groups, and hierarchies begin to develop." It's at this stage you find that some children blend into "cool" groups, while others take longer to find their groups, or float around the periphery. This stage of development is completely normal, but it's not easy for those left out.

Nancy Rue, a teacher-turned-author who wrote the Mean Girl Makeover trilogy, said, "Teenage boys and girls handle friendships differently. While boys value their friendships, they're not the potentially devastating things they can be for girls, who tend to over-analyse and emotionally invest more than boys. This means they suffer more when those friendships go wrong."

With that in mind, how can we help our daughters navigate those classroom clashes? Social media has changed the bullying landscape quite a bit since I was a kid – so what's a parent to do?

While it's tempting to reassure your teenager that not being invited to a party isn't the end of the world, it's better to acknowledge that, in their world at least, it can be. "If your daughter is having problems with her friends, don't tell her not to worry, to get over it or to grow up and just get along with each other," says Rue. "Instead, let her see you take her concerns seriously, while also helping her to have some perspective. So, say, 'You haven't been invited and that must feel awful. I get it.' Girls confide in their parents less as they approach thirteen or fourteen but showing her you understand will encourage her to confide more." As parents, we need to be there to listen when friendships go awry. It can be hard to witness at times but, as adults, we know that they'll eventually find those friends that are always worth the wait.

Clinical psychiatrist and award-winning journalist Irene S. Levine says, "The biggest group in any class is the one in the middle – the bystanders who see the bullying and do nothing. But they are a powerful force and can really help the kids who are being picked on, so teach your daughter to always be kind, compassionate and to stand up for others."

I spoke to Professor Phillip Slee, a Professor of Human Development in the School of Education at Flinders University in Adelaide, South Australia. He is also a trained teacher, registered psychologist and the director of the Student Wellbeing & Prevention of Violence (SWAPv) research centre.

Professor Slee has published extensively in the field of child development, bullying, school violence and stress, and he has produced educational resources in the form of videos and resource packages. I came across Professor

Slee's work online last year, where I saw a promotion for his PEACE Pack – an intervention programme that provides a framework for schools to address bullying and violence. The "PEACE" in PEACE Pack stands for:

P   Preparation: preparation and consideration
     of the nature of bullying
E   Education: education and understanding
     of the issues
A   Action: action taken and strategies developed
     to reduce bullying
C   Coping: coping strategies for staff, students
     and parents
E   Evaluation: evaluation, review and celebration
     of the programme

I asked Professor Slee to open up the conversation with me on how unkind behaviour, such as bullying, works with girls. Of course, boys also have to deal with bullying, but I wondered how it works among groups of girls.

Professor Slee said that girls tend to lean more towards relational goals than boys. These are goals that are based on the relationships you have with people or things, such as your best friend, body image or money. Boys tend to select more control goals, meaning they create goals based on what they want to have control over. This loosely indicates that girls are more socially oriented. When turning to the topic of bullying, a girl's bullying style is likely to come out as socially manipulative behaviour, whereas, in contrast, a boy will use more verbal and physical behaviours. Professor Slee says that these types of conflict can impact self-esteem and overall confidence, particularly among girls, because the majority of their bullying conflicts are played out at an emotional and social level.

I asked Professor Slee about how difficult it is for us to get girls to believe in themselves, when others don't. He replied, "In our Australian research, we found that girls initially respond to indirect aggression with confusion. However, as is the case with other forms of victimisation, girls certainly experience a range of negative psychological effects, including anxiety, loss of self-esteem and depression. This pain leads to a desire to escape through leaving the group or the school."

This leads me to discuss the topic of hurtful behaviours outside the classroom walls – specifically cyberbullying, which seems to be a monster of a concern on its own. We hear too many upsetting stories of a single image that has been forwarded to innumerable people. Smart girls are being lured into a perverted circle of trust, where they believe that what they post online will not be misused, and it's not okay. To make matters worse, people can hide behind multiple, unidentified profiles, maintaining anonymity and making it harder for the victim to defend against – and worse – escape from or stop the behaviours. Furthermore, evidence from Professor Slee's research suggests that a large proportion of those who engage in cyberbullying behaviours do so against individuals who are considered *their friends*. At this crucial point, I can only imagine it's really important for our girls to know who their friends really are. The ones who have got your girl's back, no matter what. A true friend will always have your best interests at heart.

The #MeToo Era

Professor Slee's research indicates that victimisation of girls by school peers is an everyday occurrence. Hearing stories of bullying that extend to mocking someone's appearance or sexual reputation seem to hit the very heart of what's happening for students. The sexualisation of young girls is an ongoing problem, which is leading to myriad more problems, particularly concerning our girls' mental health.

Sexualisation is everywhere, from TV programmes and movies to video games and marketing campaigns. Girls feel pressured by society to be more attractive. All of a sudden, our little girls seem to be pouting in the mirror or flicking their hair. We wonder where this stems from until we realise it's all around us. What one person considers to be harmless fun can be looked at as the sexual victimisation of girls.

As a mother of two boys in the #MeToo era, it's important for me to raise my boys to value girls and not judge them by how they look or how "sexy" they are. Teenage boys can feel under pressure to act "like a guy", which can mean fitting into a certain view of manhood. I know it won't be long until my older son becomes a teenager and is exposed to the pressures of peer groups and cultural messages, not to mention the hormones. I hope he'll still sit with me and talk openly about equality and gender boundaries. I'm raising a girl who is confident, resilient and believes in her own abilities. I'm also busy raising two boys who need to be strong, empathic, kind and need to understand how to challenge misogyny and sexism in this new world.

Professor Slee highlights the influence of peers as role models for our children. In schools and online settings, peers are often the first group turned to by our kids when negative situations arise, such as bullying. Teachers and parents should encourage young people to choose someone they trust when they want to talk about something distressing, or if they find themselves being bullied. Here is some advice from Professor Slee about how to help children deal with bullying:

- Secrets grow and spread in the dark, but if brought into the light, they shrink and become less harmful.
- Be aware that for many mental and wellbeing issues there is shame and embarrassment attached. Encouraging the young person to "just talk" to someone might not be enough.
- Having just one good friend is a protective cloak, so developing friendships at school and at home should be a priority.
- Parents and teachers can be good role models, demonstrating socially competent behaviour, for example, conversation skills, empathy and kindness.

What can parents do to help kids build a safe and reasonable relationship with social media before they go out on their own? Social media, at times, can feel more like a trap than anything else. The power of a visual image is so strong that it almost sucks us in. We often go down a rabbit hole, scrolling through Instagram and, before we know it, we've lost so much time we could have spent doing something else. Not only is it addictive for us, it's addictive for our children too.

When it comes to a healthy social media habit for our teen girls, much of it comes down to discipline and healthy behaviours. It's not about taking the device away or just having one conversation about it. That won't deal with the real issues.

I spoke to Molly Gunn, the brains behind Selfish Mother, the popular web platform that enables "like-minded friends" to share "what us parents are really thinking". On the website, members can post blogs to be shared with the rest of the community. Selfish Mother boasts 10,000 readers a day, 4,500 writer users and has clocked up more than 133,000 Facebook likes and more than 100,000 Instagram followers. I thought Molly would be a great person to chat to about social media – both the ups and the downs.

—

Bullying is not About You; It's About Them
by Molly Gunn

I used to be a fashion journalist and I worked with several publications before going freelance. I've worked for many newspapers and women's magazines, but when I had a child, I decided I needed to look after myself so I could look after my son. I started the blog Selfish Mother because otherwise I was going to go completely insane. It was around this time that the "perfect mother" myth was going around, suggesting that we're meant to bake cupcakes and completely give ourselves over to raising our kids.

In 2013 I started the blog, writing posts about my experiences, but also inviting other writers to write blogs on travel and such. First person pieces were gaining a lot more attention, so I put more on Facebook, growing my audience to 1,000 people. It grew organically by others

"Encourage girls
to gain happiness
from just being
themselves, as
opposed to how
they look."

MOLLY GUNN

sharing posts, and, the more content I shared, the more engagement I received. Before starting my Instagram account, I had around 40,000 followers on Facebook.

At this time, I had started a clothing line, with T-shirts and sweatshirts raising money for women going to war, and so everything I was doing was very real. My audience grew, with mothers wanting to share my experiences and contribute to the charities by purchasing my clothing line. I always spoke about real motherhood and real life. Being honest, open, authentic and supportive of others really grew my social media. By the end of 2018, we'd raised over £1 million, spread across about ten different charities, including Stand Up to Cancer and Prostate Cancer UK.

On social media, it's often difficult to deal with the comparisons to others. Personally, I feel like I'd always managed to avoid that feeling of being concerned about my figure or weight growing up. I realise this is because my mum was never obsessed with those things either; she never fretted over her looks. There was never an obsession with looks in our household, and I grew up being comfortable in myself.

I have really frizzy hair, and I didn't learn to tame it until my twenties. I used to look back and wonder why my mum didn't help me out with it as a kid, but now I'm grateful because I was never primed to look a certain way – and that's a good thing. I had a chance to just be myself and focus on other things in life. I wish we could encourage girls to gain happiness from just being themselves, as opposed to how they look.

Comparing yourself with others is a natural preoccupation, but trying to encourage children to follow accounts with empowering women, instead of beauty *accounts, is so beneficial. Lead by example. By feeling worthy in yourself, you can encourage your children to feel worthy. Give love and positive energy at home. I want my kids to be led by a good example. I've recently started doing more exercise, and I hope that will rub off on my kids. I don't worry about my looks, but I'm empowered by my body and enjoying it.*

We need to reinforce what's great about our daughters, but also encourage them to channel their energy into things that will engage their mind. People will always be weird or mean, but my personal motto is "kill with kindness". It's hard to develop a thick skin but if someone says a negative comment about you, it definitely says more about them.

Social media isn't healthy for self-esteem, and the way these pages work can lead to unhealthy habits. If you start getting rid of the things you don't like seeing on Instagram and liking the things that empower you, social media can become a positive place. However, leaving social media to its own devices can be quite worrying in terms of mental health – especially for those new to social media.

Generally, on social media, I have a supportive audience. However, when I do receive a negative comment, I just delete it. I don't want to respond to negativity because I don't want to encourage it, and I don't want negativity in my feed. Someone did once message me saying, "You talk s*** and your lipstick is too bright," to which I actually responded, "Thanks! Thanks so much for sharing that." I've also been trolled, with someone posting pictures of my designs, and eventually my husband and my house. She messaged a lot of my Instagram followers to tell them how awful I was, which I just put down to someone being very strange. I tend to ignore it.

Recently, I made an Instagram video (IGTV) to explain to my followers that the comments and messages aren't always nice, but if you haven't got anything nice to say, don't say it at all. That IGTV got a very large following, with thousands of comments. Negativity doesn't need to be spread and it doesn't deserve your energy in justifying yourself. Be secure enough in yourself to know that the problem doesn't lie with you – it lies with them.

Friendships are so hard. I used to keep a diary, and often I would list my friends, and note down those I no longer liked. Friendships in school are ever-changing and so complicated – and it can really negatively affect your day when friendships aren't working well. One way of dealing with this is just by being your best self. Be as kind as you can, and as honest as you can. If someone upsets you, it doesn't mean you've done something wrong, it can simply be that they've had a bad day too. Here's what I would recommend:

- *Don't resort to gossiping – never stoop to someone else's level.*
- *Hold your head high – don't let others get you down.*
- *Talk to someone – sharing a problem can halve a problem.*
- *Have an outlet – whether that's writing a diary or going out and doing your favourite thing.*

I want my daughter to be a girl who knows she can do anything she wants. However, I also want her to know that it's okay to not be a high-achiever – so long as she's happy and confident in herself. I want her to not get too hung up on her body image, and I know the best thing I can do for her is to be the best example. As a parent I can only be the person I want her to be when she's older.

———

Being a parent isn't easy, and both Professor Slee and Molly Gunn have opened up the conversation on some tough topics, including bullying and trolling. Despite the noise and external pressures our girls face every day, we must teach them that they have the power to change things. To make a difference. We have to stand up and use our voice to say what is acceptable behaviour and what's not.

This is where it becomes vital for parents, caregivers and role models to talk to our girls about consent. If you have any concerns, or you sense any changes in your daughter's behaviour, it's important to open those channels of communication. This all starts with trust. Discussing tough topics openly with your daughter before they're exposed to them can be really healthy. Furthermore, it could really help them act responsibly if there's a time when that situation arises.

There are highs and lows as our girls navigate the journey of their teenage years, but our girls shouldn't feel overburdened. They should be given permission to enjoy their childhood and the security it brings. Part of that security is finding the right friends. A good friend will help your daughter feel more secure and ensure she has someone to support her and listen to her, in addition to her parents or caregivers.

For our girls, every friend – lifelong or short-lived – will play an important role in some part of her life, whether she realises it or not.

Despite the
noise and external
pressures our girls
face every day, we
must teach them
that they have the
power to change
things. To make
a difference.

Seven Smart Ways to Support Your Girl

When researching friendships, social media and mental health, I became more conscious of how those three components are intertwined. I came across a psychologist called Dr Donna Wick, the founder of Mind to Mind Parent, whose work spans these areas. As a mother of three grown-up daughters herself, I thought she would be a brilliant person for me to connect with.

Upon looking further into her work, I discovered that, sadly, she passed away in 2017. This made me feel more determined to include her words of wisdom in this book – to celebrate the career she built around her love for parenting and based on her fascination with the human mind. Dr Wick had five key messages that she wanted to impart. I would like to share them here because I find them incredibly insightful. The final two thoughts on the list are my own, which I feel complement Dr Wick's advice.

1. **Monitor social media carefully**
   Don't underestimate the role social media plays in the lives of teenagers, warned Dr Wick, who said, "The power of a visual image is so strong. It's disorienting." Many teens never knew a world where social media didn't exist, and for them the things that happen online – slights, break-ups, likes or negative comments – are very real. When you talk about social media, make sure you're really listening and be careful not to dismiss or minimise your teen's experiences.

2. **Encourage them to think outside the box**

Dr Wick said, "When you talk to your child about social media, encourage her to explore it in a more critical way. A great way to start is to try asking her what she thinks has been cropped or edited out of her friends' 'perfect' pictures and why. That can lead to larger questions: Do you think your friends are really the people they appear to be online? Are you? What's the purpose of posting a photo? What is it about getting 'likes' that feels good? Does looking at social media affect your mood?"

3. **Help them understand that failure is part of learning**

Dr Wick reinforced the importance of giving our daughters a healthy message that it's okay to fail. She said, "Encouraging parents to share their own failures with kids is a good thing. Show them examples of when things didn't work out for you as planned, or when a project went wrong, as they will really welcome the opportunity to hear your story. Our girls need to see that failure is part of how we learn to succeed and there is no shame in picking yourself up, dusting yourself down and trying again."

4. **Praise (and show) effort**

Dr Wick said that remembering to praise your child when they have worked hard on something, no matter what the outcome, can make a difference to their self-esteem. Wick talked about why we should share our own stories with our girls – the times we've had successes and the times when we've tried but failed. She said, "It's helpful to examine how comfortable you are showing your own efforts, especially those that don't end in success. Being proud and open about your own work sets a powerful example for your child."

5. **Recommend a social media mini-break**

Encourage your daughter to delete the apps she needs a short break from. It's so easy to remove them and add them again later. Taking a short break from some social media apps can be a brilliant way to rest and recharge your mind in a healthy way. I have many friends who are adults, who enjoy doing this too! Dr Wick's advice is, "If you're asking your child to take a break, practise what you preach and pledge to stay off media as well. It can be every bit as hard for parents to unplug as kids."

6. **Talk to your daughter**

There has been a rise in unsettling content posted on social media. Even with parental restrictions, sometimes this content can slip through. We can't hover over their shoulders to watch everything they see, but we should make sure to remind our girls that if they see something that unsettles or upsets them, it's really important that they talk to us about it. Remind her that you're glad she reached out to you and that she should never be afraid to do so.

7. **Go filter free**

Remind your daughter that, often, many of the photos she will see online are filtered. That means some people may be heavily editing their face or body to look different. However, remind her that she doesn't need to follow this pattern, and that when we post unedited, unfiltered versions of ourselves, we are learning to accept our own inner beauty.

Conversation 7: "We lost another game. Maybe I should quit."

American industrialist Henry Ford once said, "The only real mistake is the one from which we learn nothing." Of course, our girls would much rather see a piece of homework covered in ticks than crosses. Our girls love praise and the feeling of accomplishment – I think we all do – but, equally, we know that there is a steep learning curve to navigate when things go wrong.

From the age of four, my daughter did ballet after school. I can't recall whether it was her idea or mine (probably mine). Dance was such an enjoyable part of my childhood, even though I was pretty dreadful at it. For a few years, she seemed to enjoy it, but our Erin is no ballet dancer. She would openly admit that herself. She was more like a heavy-footed elephant than a light gazelle floating across the room. Term after term, I started to notice her interest in dance was declining. There was no enjoyment, no spark there anymore. Subsequently, on more than one occasion she said, "Mama, I don't want to do ballet anymore. Can I stop it now?" By the age of six, she was doing Taekwondo and rugby instead – and she loved them both! These ended up being much more suited to her personality.

We talk a lot in this book about giving things a try. I keep coming back to this point because of how important it is. It's good for us to push ourselves out of our comfort zones at different stages of our life. However, what happens when we try something new that doesn't quite go to plan? When is the right time to quit?

The word "quit" just sounds negative, so it can be difficult to turn quitting into a positive thing. Can something positive come from a negative? I'm hoping that, through our next contributors, we might be able to explore this question more.

At the end of the day, most of us want to feel happy and fulfilled. We want our children to feel this too, which means we must give ourselves – and them – the space to work out what happiness and fulfilment looks like.

Over and over, we get told to "carry on" or to "finish what we started", so when kids quit, it can be seen as a bad thing by others. After all, sticking with something when it's difficult or uncomfortable can teach perseverance, discipline and confidence – all important skills to carry with us into adulthood, and qualities that I've advocated earlier on in this book. But you can't apply one attitude to every situation. Here, I could see Erin was right. Ballet was just not for her.

But then something else happened.

My daughter had joined Rainbows in Girlguiding UK, followed by Brownies. This had lasted a few years until, once again, the conversation reared its head another time. "I'm really not enjoying Brownies anymore, Mum." Erin went on to explain that the Brownies spend quite a lot of time in the village hall, which involves craft-type activities, and, quite honestly, that's just not her. She craves being outside. Week after week she had continued to show up for Brownies, but whatever spark had first been there for her was now missing. I thought about how long it may have taken her to find the confidence to tell me she wasn't enjoying it anymore.

I was proud of her for drawing her own conclusions on what was right for her. On a personal level, and perhaps selfishly, I didn't want her to quit Brownies. They were such a lovely bunch of girls and volunteers. But on the other hand, why should she continue if she wasn't enjoying it anymore? Is it really in our kids' best interests to see every commitment through to its bitter end? And what if we flipped that question on its head and asked if there might be equally valuable qualities to be gained by learning to let go of the things that aren't right for us?

Knowing When to Say No

Quitting carries plenty of stigma, even for adults, and figuring out when it's the best choice for our children is complex. As parents and caregivers, I believe we have a duty of care to check in with our children at the start of each season and check interest levels and motivation levels are still there. Gathering insights at the beginning of the term can be useful in understanding possible changes later down the line.

Things have changed a huge amount since I was a girl. The choice of extracurricular activities for our kids has grown to an epic scale. There's so much to do, it's almost hard to decide what to choose or prioritise. As a result, some kids are exhausted. We recently dropped gymnastics from Erin's weekly schedule too. Not because she wasn't enjoying it, but just because she was too tired. On that occasion, it was me, as her parent, following a gut instinct, that drove that decision. My daughter didn't want to stop gymnastics but, in turn, once we had sat down together to talk about it, she agreed it was the right decision. Something had to give. Talking it through with my daughter in advance was the best way for us to come to a joint, healthy decision that we felt was right for her and her needs.

My friend's son recently gave up his Sunday rugby despite being pretty good at it. However, she said the change for them as a family has been completely liberating. That didn't mean he'd given up sports completely, but, instead, she said he could focus on a different sport that he was *more* passionate about. He was still continuing with a different sport, so he was still getting the all the benefits of participation, teamwork and regular exercise.

The moral of this story is that, yes, it is important to follow things through but, at any age, there's a big difference between working hard towards something you truly care about and toiling over something your heart just isn't in. Perhaps this is why so many adults are taking the plunge, quitting a job they just don't enjoy anymore and using the opportunity to start their own venture.

We talk so much about the power of saying yes, but as my friend, Olympic athlete Michelle Griffith-Robinson, reminds me, saying no can be strong and empowering too. As my daughter gets older and takes her own journey into the teenage world, I want her to feel confident that she can exit a path, a job or even a relationship that isn't right for her. If we start something, should we feel obligated to finish it at any cost? Even if it makes us unhappy?

I'm not saying that our girls should just quit thoughtlessly. Ultimately, we want to make room for our girls' interests and passions to evolve – whatever they may be. Who knows which passions will become a core purpose for them that could end up being a big part of their lives? The important aspect here is to give our girls the space and guidance so they can personally decide what happiness and fulfilment looks like for them.

In some situations, quitting is simply the right thing to do. It could clear the path for your daughter to do something else that she loves – and that should be embraced as a good thing.

The Olympic Games present a great opportunity to inspire our next generation in so many positive ways. It might sound cheesy, but a "can do" approach and putting in the maximum effort is the attitude we want to instil in our children. Watching the Olympics, it's clear to see that everything is in the preparation. This is not something that has happened overnight. Olympic athletes often talk about their years of gruelling training and all the sacrifices they've made – all for this moment. How amazing must that feel when it pays off?

This led me to think about those who persevere. The ones who don't give up, but who still know when the time is right to throw in the towel. I wondered how it must feel to be an Olympic athlete at the top of your game and then making the decision to retire. Everything around you that you have ever known will have to change.

Michelle Griffith-Robinson is an Olympic athlete who represented Great Britain for over two decades in the triple jump. Michelle joins only a handful of women in the UK to have jumped more than 14 metres. Michelle has had her fair number of ups and downs during her professional career, including a painful injury in 2005, when she snapped her Achilles tendon in South Africa.

The road to recovery was tough on Michelle's body, but even more difficult mentally. There were days when she wanted to simply give up. Her husband, who was her strength and conditioning coach at the time, kept saying, "You don't want to be remembered for giving up from this injury." She did keep going, and she shares her story with us in this chapter.

After retiring from professional sport, Michelle became a successful personal trainer with several high-profile clients, including Spice Girl Mel B. Nowadays, she counts me as a loyal client, and we train two or three times a week. A wife and mother of three, Michelle now spends much of her time helping others through coaching and mentoring. She is a lead mentor for the Dame Kelly Holmes Trust, as well as being an ambassador for Diabetes UK and Women's Aid.

———

Tomorrow is Another Day
by Michelle Griffith-Robinson

I started my career in sport at just eleven years old. I had three older brothers who were really sporty, so I was surrounded by sport from a young age. Even my mum loved her fitness classes. It was at one of her fitness classes, where I had tagged along, that my mum gave me one pound to go and join the athletics club while she did her workout.

I was a long-legged, tall Black girl with a big afro puff and a strong ability to run. Running in a club was the start of me finding a tribe, a group, a hobby that I committed to, and that turned out to be my career – and led me to become an Olympian. My mum, even to this day, still says it was the best one pound she ever invested!

By the time I was fourteen, I began trying out the long jump. It was the long jump that took me to my first Youth Olympic games in Holland, and, although I recognised that I was quite good at it, I knew I wasn't going to set the world on fire. The women's triple jump was a relatively new event, but I gave it try and, suddenly, I had found my thing, my passion. I was around eighteen years old by then.

Six years on from when I first ever set foot on an athletics track, this was the real start of my international journey – as a triple jumper. By the age of nineteen, I had broken the British record several times and set a record of 13.05 metres, which stood for nearly fifteen years. I won numerous national titles, went to every major championship, including the World Championships and the Commonwealth Games, and became the first woman to jump more than 14 metres in the Commonwealth.

I was used to winning, but I was also used to failing. I've learnt many lessons throughout my career, and failing is just another opportunity to try again. I've bombed out of big competitions and I've failed at jumps I can do with my eyes shut! Two years in a row, I received "no jumps" at the English Schools' Athletics Championships, despite being so sure I was going to win. This is no easy career, and when I've failed, I've cried like a baby. I left those competitions and I realised I'd never ever be going into a competition so certain I was going to win again. That was probably the biggest lesson I learnt. I was so disappointed because I'd let myself and my coach down, though, as my mum always said, "At least you made it there!" As a teen, you don't want to hear it, but it's important to be told: "Come back another day. Tomorrow is another day." Some of the best advice I could give is to dust yourself off, get back up and go again.

My daughter Reese went to the English Schools' Athletics Championships in 2019, and her jumps didn't go as well as she'd hoped. She told me that she felt like she had let herself down. She's still very new to the triple jump, and she said she was embarrassed at her performance. Instantly, I said to her, "You showed yourself brilliantly today." On reflection, that's not what you want to hear right then. When you aren't happy with a performance, you need to wallow in the right there and then. But in twenty-four hours' time, that's when you need the encouragement — to remind yourself that you're doing great. Try again.

Often, we find that we need time to have that reflection — to think, and to move on. We all need to reflect on everything we do. As my mum would say, "Let's talk about this tomorrow."

One of my most challenging periods was getting ready for the 2000 Olympic Games. In 1996, I came fourteenth. I did my best and left satisfied. Preparing for the 2000 Olympic Games, I trained hard despite coming back from an injury. I missed the standard by one centimetre. I did everything possible, but the wind was against me. This meant that I didn't make the 2000 Olympic Games. One centimetre between me and my dreams of the Sydney Olympic Games. I stayed in bed and cried for a week.

I was at the peak of my fitness, the best stage of my life, but it just didn't go well for me on a day when I needed it to go well for me. Despite everything inside of me that wanted to give up, I carried on again. I found an inner resilience, and I'm really proud of the fact that I did.

I continued training, and again worked incredibly hard to get myself in the best physical condition possible. In many ways I was lucky enough to have so much support around me. Then, coming into 2005, I thought, "This is it." I managed the best winter training, had the best support team, and then... snap. I literally snapped my Achilles tendon. I fell to the floor and cried with pain. It was at this point that I said to my husband, "Matt, I'm going to retire."

There were so many times I wanted to give up after that. It was the most painful journey. I literally started from scratch. After surgery, my husband said to me, "Don't retire. Don't leave it on this note. You can do better." He said, "Life is a journey – don't quit like this." I carried on, and I was selected for the Melbourne Commonwealth Games in 2006. I remind myself that if I'd given up at any of those hurdles, I would never have made it that far.

In 2006, I walked out into the stadium in Melbourne with my family for my last ever performance for England. I'd done my best, working so hard up until that point, and that day, after I looked up at my family, my husband and my mum – who worked so hard to support me – I said, "That's it, I'm done." And now, when I measure success, I measure it in the circumstances it presents itself in. I went through all the barriers, and all the hurdles. But it was so worth it.

As a life coach, a mentor and a mother of two teen daughters myself, I think self-esteem is one of the biggest things right now. We need to empower girls to believe in themselves. We need to help our girls find something they can hold onto that allows them to believe in themselves.

Over the years, I've heard so many young girls say, "I don't do sports because my face gets red," or "I don't run because I don't like getting sweaty." It's our job, as facilitators and educators, to allow teens to overcome the problems they face and show them they shouldn't stop them from performing, or even just getting involved. Self-consciousness takes over, and we shouldn't dismiss this, but we should try to find a solution for them.

As a teen, I was always very conscious of having big boobs. I hated it. I did everything I could to cover it up. But you can't help the way your body was built. Embrace the way you look and find things that help you feel better about embracing things naturally. I try to be a role model to my girls. When I'm training, I look a mess – but I'm going out to train. There's a time and place for everything, and sport is not the time to look your best – and that's okay. I want them to see me sweating, because I'm proud of that.

It's also our job to make more sports available for girls to try. I think more girls would love boxing, karate or rugby, but they aren't always offered for them to try. Showcase the right role models and target the right audience. What we have right now is not enough. We need to target girls at a young age, right from the start of school. By the time girls reach their teenage years, it's often too late.

These are my top positive thoughts to pass on to our teens:

- *Love yourself first – it's not arrogance, it's love.*
- *Love your own uniqueness and walk in your own shoes.*
- *You are yourself; there are no copies of you.*
- *Don't throw hate at yourself. If you wouldn't treat your best friend that way, don't treat yourself that way.*
- *Lift yourself up and lift each other up.*
- *Just the simplest of things you can say to another girl can change her day – but compliment the natural things about her, not the superficial things.*
- *Build on your inner self-confidence.*

As a final thought, if there is one thing I'd say is the most important lesson to teach our girls, it's to remind them that they are good enough.

———

Michelle's inspiring story reminds us that children should not be afraid to fail. She sees every experience as an opportunity to learn. Her praise, "You showed yourself brilliantly today," is such a powerful, positive message that we can use with our girls every day. I, personally, will be mindful to remember to say this to Erin. Michelle reminds us that when things don't go to plan for our daughters, we can discuss with them what they could have done differently, or what they learnt from the process. This process will help them grow through the experience, and show them how to value the power of perseverance. In turn, this will encourage them to be confident enough to try again in the future and not be put off by the thought of failure.

In 2016, psychologist Angela Duckworth published *Grit*, a book about why a combination of passion and perseverance plays such an important role in achievement and overcoming setbacks. Duckworth states that helping kids have a sense of purpose is important. Some parents are busy trying to reduce the risk of failure by giving their children a competitive edge in the race for high grades. Of course, there's nothing wrong with wanting your daughter to get great grades. However, what we are suggesting here is that you don't want her pursuit of outstanding grades to blur the importance of just being herself with all the great qualities that make her unique.

I spoke to another Olympic athlete, Steve Backley OBE, about how he regularly switches up the conversations he has with his teenage daughters to take the focus off winning. For example, if his daughter wins a netball match, sometimes, instead of saying, "I'm so proud of you," he will say, "Wow – you must be really proud of yourself. How does that make you feel?"

Steve turned to the javelin after initially starting out in athletics as a cross-country and middle-distance runner. Twenty-five years later, he's the four-time European javelin champion and has won the Commonwealth Games three times. Steve is also the first British athlete to have medalled at three consecutive Olympic Games. He made the world top ten every year from 1989 to 2004 and has been world number one on three occasions.

In 2004, at the age of thirty-six, Steve rounded off a great career by taking fourth place at the Olympic Games in Athens. Although this was his lowest Olympics positioning, it illustrates the consistency of his performances throughout his competitive career at major championship level. Now an author and a speaker, Steve is also the co-founder of BackleyBlack and Perform in Property.

I wondered how an Olympic athlete of Steve's calibre would help his teenage girls navigate the ups and downs of life.

———

Shift Your Mindset
by Steve Backley OBE

Choosing good role models is really important as it helps girls learn how to adopt the right mindsets and behaviours for personal growth. Inspiring role models encourage our girls, not only to believe in themselves, but to expand on the point of what's possible when we do. Helping our girls look for truly successful people can encourage all of us to be a better version of ourselves.

Both my daughters have a true passion for netball and, in this instance, Pamela Cookey has been hugely influential for my daughters. Pamela has played and captained some amazing games for England Netball, and is a top-class goal shooter. If I ever get the chance, I call Pamela on the mobile when I'm in the car with the girls and their faces just completely light up at the sound of her voice. Her positivity and energy are infectious. Naturally, I appreciate that not everyone has access to sporting role models like Pamela on their phones, but using this as an example, you might be surprised by the influential role models you can find in your contacts list.

Positive role models can be a building block for greater self-esteem. However, it's important to remember that self-esteem needs to be balanced. Having self-awareness and a really accurate representation of self can help build a balanced self-esteem in young girls.

I was first introduced to the work of Carol Dweck about ten years ago. For those who haven't heard of her, she's an American psychologist known for her work on mindsets. Carol has spent much of her career diving into why people succeed (or don't) and what's within our control to foster success. Her theory of the two mindsets – fixed and growth – and the difference they make in outcomes is incredibly powerful.

Changing our beliefs can have a powerful impact. The growth mindset creates a powerful passion for learning. In Carol's bestselling book, Mindset, she writes, "Why waste time proving over and over how great you are, when you could be getting better?"

In a TED Talk viewed more than one million times, Carol Dweck talks about the power of "Yet". She shares this story: "I heard about a high school in Chicago where students had to pass a certain number of courses to graduate, and if they didn't pass a course, they got the grade 'Not Yet'. And I thought that was fantastic, because if you get a failing grade, you think, 'I'm nothing, I'm nowhere.' But if you get the grade 'Not Yet', you understand that you're on a learning curve. It gives you a path into the future."

I followed a method when coaching years ago, developed by the psychiatrist Elisabeth Kübler-Ross. She was a pioneer in near-death studies and she created a theory of the different stages of grief/change, also known as the Kübler-Ross model. My method was based on her model, and included the following four stages:

Denial (refusal of change)
Resistance (I get that, but it doesn't apply to me)
Exploration (asking questions; starting to understand)
Commitment (accepting change; focusing on the future)

In any change – grief or not – we will go through these stages. We can't expect to jump from denial to commitment – that leads to unhealthy commitments. In understanding these processes of change, we can help teenage girls who are going through change to accept their emotions and behaviours, enabling our girls to build a better sense of self at the same time.

1 Denial	2 Resistance
Change doesn't sink in Disbelief/numbness Withdrawal Question the change Work as usual	Negativity/pessimism Expression of emotions Focus on personal impact Absences increase Productivity dips
3 Exploration	**4 Commitment**
Experiment/take risks Seek information/answers Generate new ideas Distractions/stress Uncertainty/excitement	Feel comfortable with the change/accept new roles Focus on the future Set new goals Build action plans

These stages of change come up in every change a person makes, from a decision as small as getting her haircut, to one as large as that transition between primary and secondary school. If your teen has something on her mind, it can be useful to understand her emotions and behaviours in terms of which stage she may be at – and then aid her slowly to the next stage. Working through this model provides structure.

It's more about listening to what your daughter is saying, as opposed to asking her the next question. Listening to your teen is one of the most important things you can do for them. Around 60–70 per cent of what we say comes across through body language, 20 per cent from intonation, and therefore only a tiny piece of what we say comes from the words we use. Actively listening to your daughter and listening out for her needs is more important than conveying the right message through words.

Emotional intelligence is essential if you want to have a meaningful conversation with another person. To be emotionally intelligent, we must be aware that body language says so much more than the words coming out of your mouth. These are five components of emotional intelligence, according to psychologist Daniel Goleman:

- *Self-awareness*
- *Self-regulation*
- *Internal motivation*
- *Empathy*
- *Social skills*

If we can find these five components in ourselves, we are in a good place.

When you can't change the direction of the wind – adjust your sails. We often get ourselves worked up over things we can't control. Smart people will work with things they can control and not worry about the things they can't. Know that whatever is happening to you right now, "this too shall pass." The most successful way to see the light at the end of the tunnel is to surround yourself with positive people. As parents, we should strive to be positive around our teens – but also encourage our teens to surround themselves with positive peers. Peer groups have a potentially large influence on who your daughter becomes.

Too many people focus on the negative aspects of themselves. As parents, our role is to hold up the mirror. My teenage daughters are more likely to change due to an experience than because of what I say. My role is to say, "How does that make you feel?", "What does that mean?" or "Tell me more," rather than, "Don't do that, don't say that."

Self-esteem is an essential part of healthy development – and that's something we all recognise. Having good self-esteem starts with self-awareness: who am I, where am I? Deep, soul-searching questions and having a really precise understanding of who you are, are integral to developing self-esteem. One thing I've learnt is that comparing ourselves to others can be one of the biggest pitfalls to developing self-esteem. I used to walk into a room and wonder if people like me. Now I walk into a room and wonder if I'll like them.

"I used to walk into a room and wonder if people like me. Now I walk into a room and wonder if I'll like them."

STEVE BACKLEY OBE

There are multiple practices that can build self-esteem and self-belief: start with an awareness, create a set of goals, give yourself permission to slowly merge who you are into who you want to be. Many young girls have a fixed mindset that they were born with low self-esteem, and therefore will always have low self-esteem. We need to encourage an acceptance of control – the understanding that growing self-esteem is in your control. This is the most significant shift of all and allows teenagers to explore new ideas.

———

We can learn a huge amount from Olympians, and Steve is no exception. Olympians have this incredible growth mindset, the mentality that they can always improve, always go further. This growth mindset is what encourages us to "reach for the sky", or "go for gold", in the case of athletes.

Going for gold is an obsession for athletes, and the Olympic Games are the pinnacle of sporting achievement. So what happens when a medal isn't won? Where do Olympians go from there? What interests me is that when this happens, Olympians still come away pursuing success. They are hungry for more. Great athletes know they have done their absolute best and they take away lessons they've learnt from that experience. Knowing who they are, and believing in their own abilities, continues to drive them forward. They move on and think about the next competition, the next goal.

As Steve says, it all starts with self-awareness. Who am I? What could I be capable of? If we're going to build self-esteem and self-belief in our daughters, and encourage them to pursue their goals, then we can take some practical advice from Steve. I loved when he said, "Changing our beliefs can have a powerful impact."

Another thing we can learn from Steve and Michelle, our two Olympian contributors, is that there is a time and a place when it's okay – actually, when it's *right* – to stop, to call it a day. Knowing when that time is comes from knowing yourself and knowing that you've given it your all – and that you're proud of how far you have come.

If your daughter is in a position right now where she's not sure whether to quit something, or whether it's the right time, talk to her and ask her why she feels under pressure. Letting go of something she has been keen on, or is passionate about, isn't easy. Knowing when it's time to give up can be hard, especially when she's trained and persevered to achieve a goal.

Ask your daughter to write down the reasons she wants to quit. Answering that question for herself is an important part of the process. Furthermore, writing down the pros and cons may help her make her decision. On a positive note, freeing herself may open the door to let her focus her attention on a different goal that's fresh and exciting. I hadn't really considered this before, but I've realised that quitting could actually feel like a very courageous thing to do.

"Failing is just another opportunity to try again."

MICHELLE GRIFFITH-ROBINSON

Seven Practical Ways to Deal with Failure

Michelle said that, "failing is just another opportunity to try again." However, to our girls, I know that failure can feel like a hard pill to swallow. Perhaps we can change our girls' perception of failure by looking at ways to view mistakes or failures as a path to personal success?

1. **Take responsibility**

   Whatever hasn't gone to plan, dwelling on the situation or focusing on who messed up hardly ever helps. Encourage your girls to take stock, get a hold of the situation and separate mistakes from faults. This will help your daughter regain control if she's feeling riddled with guilt.

2. **Teach her how to bounce back**

   If a project didn't work out or she didn't get picked for the team or group she wanted, remind her that there may be more opportunities ahead. Talk about what she may be able to do differently next time, or work together on how she can improve a particular skill that she really enjoys.

3. **Asking for feedback**

   Often, we're afraid to ask for feedback but, in my view, it is important. When we find out our girls have missed their place on the course they wanted or they didn't get the job they were applying for, it can be useful to know why. It takes courage, but encourage her to ask for feedback. It will help her gain useful information on what areas need to be worked on, and it's how we can constantly improve.

4. **Remind her how far she has come**

   A moment of reflection is such a useful thing. I barely remember to do it myself, but, when I sit down with my daughter and we talk through the amazing things she has done in her life so far, a warm smile appears on her face. Find the time to recognise and celebrate how great your girl is doing and remind her how far she has come.

5. **Tackle the topics she fears**

   Most girls would rather do anything than tackle the subject or project they find difficult. Maybe they spend hours avoiding homework on a certain topic, or they choose to clean their rooms before sitting down to practise their musical instrument. Encourage your daughter to tackle it head on. A few extra hours studying the things she finds hard will help your daughter improve.

6. **Show her that great things can start small**

   Many of us know the saying, "Slow and steady wins the race." Even if progress can sometimes seem slow, teach your girls that it's progress nonetheless. Great things can happen for our girls when we start with small steps. When she sets herself smaller, manageable goals she's more likely to keep going. Remember to talk to her about how good it feels to accomplish something that you've worked toward.

7. **Remind her that she showed herself brilliantly today**

Applauding effort is an important step on the road of perseverance, which will help your daughter pursue a goal or passion over time. Michelle Griffith-Robinson tells her daughters, "You showed yourself brilliantly today," which reminds her girls to keep working towards their goals. So say something similar to your girls. Show them how impressed you are when they work really hard in pursuit of something they're passionate about.

Chapter 4

THE POWER OF SELF-BELIEF

How to help our girls learn to believe in themselves every day. Reminding them that, instead of dwelling on their imperfections, they should focus on all the great things they can do.

I remember asking my daughter when she was around seven years old if she believed in herself. Her answer always stuck with me. Mostly, because I expect many of us feel the same. She said, "I believe in myself sometimes, but not all the time."

When I go into schools to deliver my talks, I often say, "Believing in yourself is not a cliché; it's an economic strategy." I say it because the quote is accurate and – more than that – our girls desperately need to hear it. When someone says you need to believe in yourself, it can sound cheesy. Perhaps you might even feel like cringing when you say it to your daughter. But the reality is that, if our girls have no self-belief, they will struggle to reach their goals. If they feel self-doubt, self-criticism or a constant feeling of unworthiness, then our girls may not be happy.

You see, in my opinion, even at our age, as parents, self-doubt and self-criticism are still there. They are always there. It's just that the self-confident part of us remembers to stand up for us and silence the noise. We have to remind ourselves that it is mainly the internal talk that's noisy. In fact, when I was recently speaking to a woman called Lucy Baker on her podcast, *The Confidence Rooms*, I had written down some notes before we started recording. One note read: "The confidence to believe in ourselves is inside us all the time. We carry it with us everywhere we go. It's just a case of when we want to unlock it." I found this to be a powerful thought. It's up to our daughters to unlock their self-worth and self-confidence when they're ready to. There's no magic formula for this. They have to do it themselves, when they are ready. We're just here to guide them and hope they unlock it before the inner critic becomes too loud.

Unlocking the power becomes harder if the key is jammed – and that happens when our daughters' brains are drained. Perhaps the lock gets jammed when our girls first get that feeling of unworthiness. They start to feel stuck and unable to move forward with true confidence. The jammed lock can act as self-doubt and this is where the crisis in our girls begins.

Believing in yourself is one of the first conversations we should be having with our girls. How can you be confident if you don't believe in yourself? How can you build resilience if you never have the self-belief to give anything a try? How can you step out into the world to be your best self if you never show your best self in the first place? Helping our girls unlock their self-belief is the first step they need to take on the path to achieving their ambitions.

When raising children, no one puts out a sign to tell you that what's coming is a kid who will have big emotions. One day she might tell you she loves you, and the next, she may tell you that you're the worst parent in the world.

Some comments cut deep, but we have to take a breath and ride those emotions like a storm that will pass.

Emotions are important and, for our teen girls, we can expect buckets of them in every form.

When my daughter turns and looks at me, I realise we have a long road ahead. I will try to be ready. I will try to say the right things at the right time, but inevitably, I will make mistakes. We will both make mistakes. But if one thing's for certain, I will always do my best to help her believe in herself. I will always remind her of her internal beauty, her strengths, her kindness and all the wonderful things that make her *her*.

I hope you'll agree that I've made a strong case that believing in yourself is not a cliché. It is, indeed, an economic strategy that will help to raise the next generation of strong, confident, kind girls who become wonderful women. Women who can raise a home, raise a company, raise a country even. Women who can raise themselves and lift up others at the same time.

When I considered the concept of self-belief, a few people sprang to mind who I thought would be great to have as contributors here. The first was someone who, when I met her, I was instantly struck by. It takes a special kind of person to walk into and command the attention of a room. This woman seemed to ooze self-confidence in a way that was mesmerising but not arrogant – and that's quite a skill. Her name is Heidi Petite and we first met in 2019 while working on a skincare campaign for Neutrogena. I've thought about what Heidi was like when she was a teenager. Has she always oozed confidence or, if not, how did she find it along the way?

___

Finding Your People
by Heidi Petite

As a young girl, I was shy, I was quiet. My confidence didn't flourish for a long time, and when it did, I'm pretty sure it flourished through the friends I met. It was those friends that really brought my personality out. Your friends become your "people" – the people around you – and picking those friends who will be around you is really important for personal growth. You want to pick the people you most connect with and the people that bring out the best in you. There are a lot of friends you could choose that don't bring out the best in you at all.

Life is not a race, and we can all develop our confidence in baby steps. Once you take the first one, it's only up from there. Confidence can be built in baby steps.

When I moved to London with a friend from school, I realised I needed to find other people like me. I wanted to find people who were a bit different, who loved wearing bright colours and were into the same things as me. I decided to try to find those people online. I searched Instagram for weeks and weeks, putting together girls I thought were my type of people – if they were nice people, if they supported charity, and so on.

I showed the list to my flatmate and we started to message them all! We would say, "I love what you're doing. I'd love to meet you. We should link up."

Eventually, one by one, we all linked up, soon getting together as a group. I quickly realised that these were my people; we were all so similar but, more importantly, we all supported each other through everything. I had finally found my group – and Confetti Crowd was born. Confetti Crowd was a business idea I had. I wanted to make the first female collective in London, to support female empowerment. It was a niche market because no one was supporting just females. I wanted to show that when we support each other we can do so much better. From being around positive and supportive friends, I'd realised that we were stronger together, and it wasn't about individualism. As a group, we could achieve so much, and we weren't ever alone. It didn't matter what I wore, because the other five were wearing that too; we were in it together. I think people loved that.

I have recently learnt that 41 per cent of girls aged between seventeen and twenty-one in the UK aren't happy with the way they look and would consider plastic surgery. Sometimes I feel the same, and think, "I don't look like me." This is because social media often impresses on people that "this" is how you're meant to look.

To be honest, most days I just don't care. I think this is me. Social media has taken over people's confidence and how they judge themselves. My main advice is: it's important to remember that a lot of social media isn't real. People are only showing the best parts of their lives, and the best parts of themselves in the mirror. Remember that these girls online have the same problems you do; they just choose not to show it. Remember, what you're given is what you're given, and you just have to work with that. Once you accept that that's who you are, you're going to be stronger than every other girl out there.

Another piece of advice is to watch who you follow. I tend to only follow girls who are confident in who they are and who show the real-life versions of themselves, not just the best bits. I follow plus-size models who love themselves, and they are the strong women I look up to more than the girls who try to look like everyone else.

I was always into fashion, and I always wanted to be slightly different. I think girls should want to be different, and not strive to look like all the other girls out there. When I met the Confetti Crowd, I met more like me, and that pushed me to become even "more of me"! Whoever turned up looking the craziest that day was admired in our team. I do dress the way I feel, and my advice would be that it's good to look to your role models and admire the way they dress, but interpret that in your own way. It's important not to follow the crowd. Take your style, and yourself, and celebrate that.

Growing up, my mum was a big role model for me. She was a model, and she always had big hair and colourful jackets. She had her own style. But being a role model doesn't mean you have to be a goody-two-shoes, or that you have to follow the rules, because my mum celebrated being unique. I found role models in P!nk and Avril Lavigne, who were always on skateboards. I'm sure they probably did things they shouldn't have, but I didn't copy them for that, I just wanted to mirror their style and the confidence they radiated.

I think it's good to be afraid sometimes because that's what gives you the excitement to push yourself further. The best thing I've ever been taught is to just go for it. Don't sit and think about things because that leads to procrastination and overthinking, which leads to doubt. It's important to just go for it, to do what you set out to do — future problems can be dealt with in the future. Those problems will also never be as bad as you think.

"Take your style, and yourself, and celebrate that."

HEIDI PETITE

The second-best piece of advice I've been taught is that when you're not sure about something – whether that be a business idea or what to wear one day – if something feels off, it probably is. Follow your gut. Go for it, but if, along the way, something feels off, your gut feeling is most likely to be right.

In dealing with negativity, you've got to learn to laugh at it. People projecting negativity onto you have their own problems and you've got to feel sorry for them. Maybe they're having a bad day and that turned into a negative comment. They probably just feel bad about themselves, and that should never influence how you feel about yourself. Don't sink to their level, just move on. Learn to look past it because it can't stop you doing what you like to do. Lean on your friends. Your group will help you be there for yourself, and if someone says something negative to me, they're saying it to all my friends too.

You've got to search for things in life; they don't just come to you. You need to put yourself out there. I was so scared to, but I massively put myself out there, messaging people who were big influencers, with 20,000 followers, asking them to be my friend! Don't be intimidated by things – go out and meet new people that give you confidence and boost you up.

With me, my style spoke for itself. At school we had dress-down week, and every day I would wear a different coloured suit. I made things my own. I went in, being myself from the start, and from that I was able to be who I wanted to be. Eventually I was kicked out of sixth form because they didn't like the way I dressed. I left, I went to college, and suddenly I was able to embrace myself even more. You do have to be who you are, and express that because eventually it will come out anyway. There's no point in trying to be someone else.

As girls, we often focus on the things we aren't so good at, but not those we are good at. It wasn't until I was in my twenties that I realised what I actually really wanted to do, which was pursuing a career in music and art. And that was something I was naturally good at. I dropped out of university, and I felt like I'd let myself down, but just six months later, I realised I had made the best decision. I'd felt an instinct and I had to go for it without thinking too much.

Making mistakes and learning through them is all part of the journey. Still, every single week, there's something I do that I realise I didn't do too well. But then, the following week, things turned out much better because I worked around the failure. It's okay to constantly fail, until you feel the instinct that "this is it, this is the one." Failing is so important. I don't look at it as a negative thing. I think it's important to consider it as a journey.

My final words of advice are: if you haven't found your people yet, don't worry. Maybe you haven't found what you want to do yet. Educate yourself, and don't be afraid to throw yourself into something new. That will push your confidence. The more you know about something, the more confident you will be in that area.

Find that one thing to educate yourself in — love it and enjoy it. In turn, it's likely you'll meet others, and you'll find others like you. You'll find your career path. It comes from developing yourself and finding yourself. Good things don't come from comfort zones. From taking that first step out, things can only get better and better.

Remember, everything is subjective, and everybody's opinion is subjective. Some people may hate what you do, others may love it. But the only important thing is that you love it. I'll never make a song everybody loves, but if it's good for me, I'm going to sing it. If you don't believe in yourself, how is anyone else going to believe in you? It's not likely that you'll make it. You have to believe in yourself and that's when it all comes together.

I love how Heidi's self-belief came from finding like-minded people. She reinforces the message that being part of a crowd doesn't diminish your individuality but can build it up. Finding your community is important and, to do so, Heidi has shown that you must not be afraid to get out there, find your people and surround yourself with those who support and inspire you.

The relationships we choose in life are fundamental to the way we think and feel, so make sure your daughter is checking the energy of the people around her. We need to remind our girls to look for the positive people who lift them up when they need it most. Your daughter will grow in so many ways with that precious good energy surrounding her. Just like Heidi found self-belief and an important sense of belonging from choosing the right crowd, we should encourage our girls to find others with shared passions and interests. Most importantly, though, they should look for friends who share the desire to support each other.

The Power of "Yet"

Choosing good friends can give our girls real social confidence, so they aren't always worrying about what other people think. But what about the way our girls think about themselves? Do they have the self-belief to persevere, even after something doesn't go their way?

We have come across Dr Carol Dweck's concept of "Yet" already and I want to talk about it some more. It's a powerful tool for dealing with setbacks, but mostly I want to talk about it because it's an idea that proves, over and over again, that mindset is everything. Throughout this book, we've learnt that it is our minds that hold the power to what we can achieve.

When I spoke to beauty-brand expert, Jo Jones, she also mentioned the power of "Yet" and, really interestingly, shares how she uses the phrase with her own daughters. I find the concept of "Yet" so incredibly powerful. When it comes to self-belief, I want to consider how we can continue to motivate girls so they know they're on the right track, even if they're not quite there yet.

I was one of those students who had to work hard in class and if, for a moment, I started staring out of the window and dreaming bigger dreams, there would be no hope in me remembering what the teacher had said. Part of me craved to be one of the children who knew the answer as soon as the teacher asked the question. I used to watch as they would shoot their hands up in the air, but that was never me. I wish I'd known about the power of "Yet" back then. When I spoke Jo Jones, we had so many similar stories from our school days, it felt as if we were kindred spirits!

Jo Jones is one of the best brand-builders in the beauty industry, thanks to her work with Charlotte Tilbury Beauty, Victoria Beckham Beauty, Space NK, Glossier, John Frieda, Burberry and many more. After a career spent working for others – most recently a fifteen-year stint at one of the biggest fashion and beauty PR companies in the UK – Jo now works for herself as a PR and brand consultant.

Jo believes that beauty has the power to change lives. It can transform, empower and build confidence. It has the power to boost self-esteem, improve wellbeing and promote self-care and self-love – something that has become more of a focus in modern times. Alongside her day job (which includes co-hosting *The Beauty Hags*, a YouTube channel with another beauty legend, journalist Nadine Baggott), Jo has also built Beauty Banks, a grassroots charity she co-founded with her friend, the journalist and broadcaster Sali Hughes. Both women were appalled to learn of the term "hygiene poverty", which is where individuals and families can't afford to keep clean and many have to choose between eating or being clean. The duo, having first-hand experience of the surplus their industry produces, started a movement to redistribute the excess to those who need it most, donating essential hygiene products, such as sanitary provisions and deodorant. Their mission is to eradicate hygiene poverty for good because they believe that being clean is a basic human right.

Jo shares her story with us, which takes us from her school days to working alongside well-known celebrities and leading organisations on their beauty brands.

Celebrate Who *You* Are
by Jo Jones

When I was at school, I was an ordinary student. I was average. I had to work hard to get a C in anything and I found linear learning difficult and uninspiring. I hung out with a big group of girls, and we were often a little mischievous, but never really got in trouble. I struggled with the good grades; I worked hard to reach them, but they just eluded me.

At school, I wasn't good, or bad, at anything. I was a middle-of-the-road student who didn't get any attention because she didn't excel or cause trouble – so I (and lots like me) were essentially ignored and left to get on with it.

Despite my family not being readers (we didn't have a book in the house) I read avidly since I was small; I went to the library, often twice a day in school holidays, which my family didn't understand and actually found quite comical. I didn't read to escape, though – I simply loved the storytelling.

I have a sister, Jackie – she's only eleven months younger than me. Growing up, we were – and remain – extremely close. Yet, despite our closeness, we're different people with different talents, likes and abilities, which is why I think it's important to recognise girls as individuals.

When I was fifteen, I went away for the summer with a friend and I came home, six weeks later, like a different person. My confidence had grown and I felt as though I had been given the opportunity to become more independent, which I thoroughly embraced. That's when

I came into my own sense of self. For the first time, I felt like I could spread my wings.

I remember being told that I shouldn't consider A-levels. The teacher had told me that I should instead go straight into employment, which I did. I was desperately keen to move out of home, so, for me, going to work meant money, which then meant I could move out. In hindsight, I should have questioned the reasoning for her telling me that A-levels weren't an option. Did she think I wasn't capable? If I really wanted to do those A-levels I should have stood up for myself. But I wasn't prepared to do that, and I wasn't prepared to live at home for much longer, either.

So, there I was, sixteen and in full-time employment at some office a short bus ride from my house. I didn't love it (I was doing office admin) but I didn't hate it either. My co-workers were lots of fun, we had a happy vibe in the office, went out for lunches and hung out together afterwards for drinks. I've always been very sociable and I enjoy the social side of work. I love working with lots of people and feeding off their energy.

From there, I went to work in the West End as a PA at an advertising agency. I hated the commute on the Central Line but loved working in the West End. Again, I loved my co-workers, loved the social aspect of being in a vibrant, exciting, creative space — it felt like it was where I was supposed to be. I tried out lots of different roles in that agency and that's where I discovered PR. They gave me my first job in PR!

On the side of my PR job, I set up Beauty Banks with my good friend, Sali Hughes. The idea behind Beauty Banks came up during a fragrance press-launch dinner with Sali. She had just returned from Wales, where she had visited a homeless shelter. I was already very aware of food banks, and if people can't afford to eat, it's highly unlikely they can afford toothpaste, hygiene products, and so on. It was ironic; we sat at an amazing, fancy dinner with celebrities on both sides and set up a social movement to support people living in poverty. We recognised our privilege, but we also knew we were lucky to have connections with generous people and brands in our industry. From then on, that was it. We launched on Instagram in February 2018 with one single post and no followers, and from there we have grown.

Beauty Banks isn't a traditional charity business, and we work hard to ensure it's kept that way because we don't want to run a business — we want to drive change. We are homemade, hands on, a little rough around the edges, and that's us. We don't have staff, an office, overheads or a team for this and a person for that — but that suits us.

I think with girls, having two of my own, we should never discount their innate personalities. My eldest daughter, Violet, has matured very quickly for her age and is so very different to my youngest, Ivy. The girls' motivations are very different, and despite the same genetic makeup and the same home environment, they're innately very different. This is something to celebrate, not attempt to change. We could have five more daughters and each would be unique and different to the others.

Our eldest daughter is creatively bright and thinks in stories. When it comes to school, we would never put her under academic pressure because she doesn't respond well to it. We don't want to compromise her mental health and emotional wellbeing for perceived academic success. I don't live through my children, I let my children express what they really want. Sometimes kids don't want to try or can't be bothered, but I won't let them say, "I can't do this." Perseverance and resilience are so important for any child, and we should encourage them to keep going for themselves, not for anyone else, and to not give up.

As a parent, I'm never prouder than when my kids show perseverance. One day in PE, a friend said to Violet, "How are you so good at netball?" to which she responded, "I was sick of being in the B-team." Violet was in the B-team throughout primary school and worked so hard to make it to the top. This has given her so much in terms of grit and resilience. Though she was always desperate for that A-team place, the best thing for her was not to get it. All the little knockbacks you have make you more resilient, and they set you up for a more successful adulthood. When something doesn't go your way, you work for it. My husband says, "That's life." We get better because of those setbacks.

On the flipside, my eight-year-old excels in everything academic. She always gets picked as the lead in the play, and she's always chosen for those little roles of responsibility at school. Ivy is very bright, being on the "gifted and talented" register in all subjects. She needs extra. Our eldest, Violet knows this, and it gets to her. She says, "Ivy's better at this, Ivy's been chosen for that." and as a parent I try to encourage both of them to realise they each have special talents they can excel in. I will always praise them equally, and when it comes to those little things like manners, I will praise the small stuff too.

I am obsessed with Ted Talks. Dr Carol Dweck once said, in one of her Ted Talks, "I love the art of 'Not Yet'." If you are told something is wrong, it's just wrong. There's nowhere to go from there. If you are told, "That's not quite right yet," you have the space to learn and grow. That's what we all need. We always need somewhere to go, and somewhere to grow. As a family, we never say, "No, that's wrong," instead, we always encourage another try, because you just haven't got there yet.

People talk a lot about not accepting things as they are, though, actually, I think there's a lot of power in accepting the way things are. I encourage my girls to keep their eyes open – to accept things, but to keep looking for the positives. I take the time to look at things through my daughters' eyes.

As a child, I went to a state Catholic school with thirty children to a class. My voice was rarely heard. My kids, at private school, have a different story entirely. Children are so confident, and that confidence seems to wear off as we age. As a child it's acceptable to say, "I'm so good at this!" but as an adult, people would hate you for saying that. When my daughters say they're good at something I reply with, "Yes you are."

We need to encourage that self-confidence to continue throughout the teenage years because, as a teenager, all you want to do is blend in. We need to encourage everybody to find their own way to stand out and realise their own potential.

Childhood is different for everyone, and the times have changed since we were children. It's important to remember that childhood is different nowadays, and those connections between our young girls are not the same.

I would spend hours out talking to my friends, but now teens will spend hours on social media. Some things, though, haven't changed, and if I can arm my kids with good manners and the ability to empathise, I'll be happy.

If I fast forward to seeing my eleven-year-old as a teenager, I see that our children often need their friends' approval, and the last thing they want is a nagging parent. It's up to me, as the parent, to ensure that my children have a good relationship with me. I will work however hard for them to know I'll always be here. When I say, "You're my girl," Violet will say, "No, I'm my girl, Mum," and I love that.

She is who she wants to be.

Here are my top tips for raising powerful girls:

- *Don't take it personally. When your daughter is behaving badly, it's easy to see it as a reflection on you. It's not about you; it's about them.*
- *When things go wrong, let them learn, and don't try to fix it, or make it better or make it go away. Against all your will, your girls need to experience hardship. Be there for them when they go through hard times, but don't pander to their every need or they won't develop the important skills of grit and perseverance.*
- *Remember the power of "Yet". At times your girl will feel like she's failing. Tell her that her time isn't now. Don't justify failures, but accept them, and work on them. If you always win, how can you improve? How can you grow into a better person?*
- *Have humility and compassion.*

———

Jo reminds us that building a strong sense of self can be a source of power for your child. I love how Jo highlights the differences between her two daughters because it's important to remind your children of the strengths and abilities that make them who they are. Focusing on that helps Jo enable her daughters to feel good about themselves. Once again, we see how the power of "Yet" can build a healthy sense of self-confidence in our girls. It's a positive phrase that keeps them moving forward, towards a goal, allowing them to explore new subjects and hobbies without worrying about failing. Jo's parenting style is about freeing her daughters to find their own way, and allowing them to explore different activities and opportunities. By encouraging this, Jo is guiding them to stand tall and be themselves and, in turn, helping them to embrace their full potential both in and out of the classroom.

From the stories and advice from all of the contributors to this book, it's clear that building self-belief can lead to opportunities – and it's opportunities that will take us places in life. That level of self-belief enables our girls to feel that any contribution they give, inside or outside of school, is valuable. The more their self-belief grows, the more likely they are to start setting themselves goals and ambitions that will lead to them feeling a sense of pride in their accomplishments, big or small. There's nothing I love more than hearing my daughter say, "I'm just so proud of myself, Mum," because that's *her* internal voice, not mine. It never fails to make my heart swell.

Seven Steps to Building Self-Belief in our Girls

Self-belief is basically how children see themselves. Particularly what they think about themselves and their ability to achieve things. It's often tied to how much they feel loved, liked or supported by their family and peers. So many of our experiences can shape our self-belief, which is why the journey is actually more important than the destination. Through trying new things, our girls can gain self-belief, and, as parents, our role is to applaud their effort.

1. **Step 1: What's Holding her Back?**

   Try to understand what it is that's making your daughter feel low in herself. Write down what is feeding the negative thoughts or feelings in her head. Ask if something happened that made her feel this way?

2. **Step 2: Challenge her Mindset**

   Is there a way she can shrink those negative thoughts? If she can't change what has happened, is there a way to change direction?

3. **Step 3: Focus on the Positive**

   It may sound like a cliché, but focusing on the positives is really important. Start by asking her to write down two or three things that are positive about herself. Take the time to recognise and embrace the good. She can also start the day by looking at or writing down a positive affirmation.

4. **Step 4: Surround her with Positive Role Models**

   Girls can and should lift each other up. Remind your daughter to surround herself with people who make her feel good, and try to stay away from the ones who don't make her feel confident about herself, or who spend a lot of time criticising others.

5. **Step 5: Try Something New**
Naturally, we enjoy staying in our comfort zones, but incredible things happen when we try something new. Whether it's a new sport or a hobby, it's not about winning or losing, it's about having the guts to try it in the first place. Ask her to do things that make her happy and cut out the things that don't.

6. **Step 6: Set Mini-Goals**
Achievements and "small wins" are a brilliant way to build her self-belief. Encourage her to set mini-goals, which she can keep to herself if she prefers. Remind her to give herself an internal high-five every time she meets one of the goals. It might be doing something she finds challenging, or it could be something like going for a brisk walk every day. Sometimes we have to build on small wins to reach our bigger goals. Who's in a hurry anyway?

7. **Step 7: Talk it Out**
If she's really struggling with negative feelings about herself, it's important not to bottle it up. Try to get her to talk to someone she trusts or a role model in her life. If she doesn't feel comfortable talking to you, maybe encourage her to reach out to another family member or a teacher. Try the "walk and talk" strategy mentioned in conversation 2, in the previous chapter. It really helps.

Chapter 5

RAISE THEM RESILIENT

Life is never plain sailing and, for our girls, there will inevitably be struggles along the way. But these challenges can make us stronger. When our daughters worry and feel afraid, we must guide them to break through that fear barrier.

We have learnt so much from the contributors who have taken the time to share their stories and wisdom with us. We have heard amazing advice on how to navigate those tricky conversations, and how to teach our girls to find their passions, discover their confidence and go out into the world as the best version of themselves.

We have learnt that if our girls aren't putting their hands up from a young age, they risk not raising their hands in adulthood, either, missing out on that new job or big promotion. We've seen how important it is to have that willingness to try without being afraid of failure. We have learnt that all experiences have their worth. We learn so much from our setbacks and, after all, if our girls never fail, how will they learn to be resilient?

The reality of life is that, at times, things don't go as we planned. How we learn to adapt and bounce back is a hugely important foundation for our girls to have. That's why I'm focusing on resilience here, in the final chapter of the book. Life is never plain sailing and, for our girls, there will inevitably be struggles along the way. Whether it's moving homes, moving schools, difficulties at home, friendship changes or losses, some of us manage better than others. But the challenges we face in life can make us stronger — if we're able to approach them with positivity and a willingness to learn. So when our daughters worry about what they fear, we must help them break through that fear barrier.

Claire Shipman, co-author of *The Confidence Code* says, "If your daughter is always wanting to be comfortable, she's not in the right place. You've got to push her out of her comfort zone and that might be literally walking to the library, it might be ordering in a restaurant, it might be cooking an egg and messing it up 400 times. There are a million different ways to force her to use that risk-taking muscle, but if she's not doing some failing – it doesn't have to be failing her junior year, every class, but it's just 'targeted failing' – she's really not learning or more importantly, I think, building confidence." I love this quote from Claire because it's so relatable. Sometimes, just getting your daughter to walk into a restaurant first or encouraging her to ask for the bill can be the small steps she needs to build her confidence.

We must remind our girls of their strengths and help them look back at how far they have come. Life is a constant reminder that we can only control the controllables. It can be tough for our girls to accept that we can't control what happens in our lives, but we can teach them to view every event as a stepping stone to a brighter future. Reframing challenges in this manner is a powerful way for our girls to build their positive mindsets. The power of positivity will go a long way in supporting our girls on their road to success – whatever success looks like for them.

Our Girls are the Women of the Future

If I think about influential women that we see in the news, Sheryl Sandberg is one name that springs to mind. She is the COO of Facebook and bestselling author of *Lean In*, where she writes about the ambition gap all around the world. In 2012, she said, "We don't raise our daughters to be as ambitious as our sons. Last month, there were T-shirts sold at Gymboree, which is a very large chain of kids stores, that said 'smart like daddy and pretty like mommy.' Not in 1951 – last month."

So, I ask, what are we, as parents, doing that contributes to the ambition gap – and what are we doing to break it down? Do we encourage our boys and girls equally to contribute at home? Do we push our girls and boys equally to be ambitious and take risks? We must remember, we are not raising girls; we are raising confident women.

Former first lady Michelle Obama is a woman after our own hearts. In a talk at the 2016 United State of Women Summit, she specifically thanked her mother for teaching her a lesson that she says has helped her become the woman and mother she is today. "The mother that I am today is a direct result of Marian Robinson," she said. "My mom is one of the smartest people, with just plain old common sense. The thing she always said, that I do remember, is that she told me and my brother, 'I wasn't raising children. I was raising adults.'"

As our girls take the journey from teenhood into womanhood, each day they gain a little sense of self. Every new year, social media tells us to consider a "new year and a new you", but maybe it was always about the *original* you. We should help our girls embrace who they really are.

As parents and caregivers, we are under increasing pressure to raise confident, well-rounded children because we want them to be confident, well-rounded adults. We read article after article, both online and offline, telling us this. But, despite reading these articles, the question is *how* do we put this into practice? Particularly for our girls today. As I've said many times before, being a parent is the hardest job in the world. We have an overwhelming responsibility to teach our children the ways of the world.

We need to help our children learn to be kind, strong, how to stand up for themselves, how to stand up for others and, crucially, how to get up when they fall. Our children must learn to foster resilience – so much hinges on what we teach them. What words of comfort will we give our kids when they fail? And what will they learn from those experiences?

Raising a girl isn't easy, but I believe we can build confident, kind daughters by supporting them well. Guiding them to take small steps, and celebrating milestones, will help build their self-esteem. In turn, this will help our girls walk into a room without having to compare themselves to anyone else.

Confidence comes from self-belief. If we can teach our girls the value of good friendships, kindness and patience, we can give them the best start on their journeys. We can help them learn how to manage self-doubt, help them find their voice, strengthen their self-confidence and find the things they love to do. My aim, and my hope, is that *Rise of the Girl* is a powerful toolkit you can refer to when you have questions you want to answer, or when you need ideas about how to give your daughter guidance.

For my final contributor, I approached comedian Helen Thorn, one half of the Scummy Mummies. Resilience is such an important topic, which is partly why I wanted it to be the final chapter of this book, and for Helen to contribute to it.

The big question for our girls is, "What could you accomplish if you had the strength not to give up?" That question brings me joy. *What could you accomplish?* It gives me hope. Resilient children have so many qualities that should not be undervalued. Positivity, self-belief, empathy and compassion. These are all qualities we want to grow in our girls. At the heart of everything, instilling resilience can help us raise happy, confident daughters.

Helen, originally from Melbourne, Australia, moved to the UK in 2006. Helen began performing comedy in 2003 and her first gig was at The Stand in Glasgow. In more recent years, Helen is best known as one half of the comedy double-act Scummy Mummies. Together with fellow mum Ellie Gibson, she co-hosts the UK's longest-running parenting podcast and performs live shows around the country. Helen is a mum of two, and an ambassador for body positivity through her own podcast, *Fat Lot of Good*, which launched in April 2019.

———

Own Your Own Happiness
by Helen Thorn

I grew up in really rural Australia, moving to the UK when I was twenty-seven. I grew up in a very narrow-minded, small town and, though I was very creative, I was encouraged by my teachers to go for a vocational career, which favoured my mathematical ability over my creative abilities.

I'm the fourth of five children. My dad was a vicar, then a schoolteacher, so I was always close to his work. His work drove our family. My mum was a childminder, and our house was always full of children! My parents really encouraged my creativity, with lots of extracurricular activities, and though that was what I really loved, I didn't always realise I could make a career out of it.

I loved art, drama, playing musical instruments – and being in all the musicals is what makes my heart sing. I suppressed that love in order to "do the right thing" – please my parents, go to university and so on. My natural go-to is being a people pleaser, which is probably why I'm a comedian. However, I was good at sciences, so I was told, "You must do this course," and, "You must go to university." As a people pleaser, I went along with that. I went to university because I knew it would make my dad happy. As girls, and as women, we were brought up to think about others almost before ourselves, which is exactly what I did. What I love is that, nowadays, we're teaching our daughters to have a good sense of self and to do what's right for them.

When I was a child, people knew I was creative and outgoing, but I used my comedy as a defence mechanism. I was badly bullied both in primary and high school. I loved classical music and I was quite a dork. I was my own person and so I used my comedy to get people to like me, almost a strategy for survival. Lots of comedians were bullied as kids – and most comedy comes from great pain. We pull comedy from painful experiences and turn it into joy. No one wants to hear about someone's perfect life, but comedy can be a relief from imperfect lives.

I knew from a young age that creativity was what I needed. It was really championed in my house, which I know now is such a privilege. I try to encourage that in my own children; music and creativity is so important. I was also very loved by my family, and that's so important too. I knew that if I told a bad joke it wouldn't matter, because I would go home to a family that loved me.

I built my resilience over time. As a chubby child in a looks-focused culture, and with no interest in sports, I was an easy target. Kids used to comment on the way I sounded, because I was brought up to speak quite well. I just wanted to be loved, and the stage brought me that satisfaction, though the mean words always hurt.

In year nine, I had a moment where I just didn't want to be sad anymore. Without telling my parents, I rang up another school and said, "I need to move schools — can I come to yours?" I decided I was going to help myself. The school said yes, and so I went. I said to the new school's principal, when I met him, that I felt really sad and needed to make a change. I realised I was the one that needed to make myself happy. That was a big turning point in my life. I took charge of my own happiness at just fourteen years old. I don't know where that strength came from, but it hasn't left me.

I was 100 per cent happier after that. I found a better school, with better friends, and I found acceptance. My moment of bravery taught me that you don't have to put up with unhappiness — and that has driven my life, and career path, from then. The resilience I taught myself is what I hope to teach my children. As much as we want to, we can't protect our children from everything, but we can share what we've learnt with them. We grow up as people pleasers, but we must realise that we need to put ourselves first and own our own happiness. As women, it's important that we can put ourselves first.

I went off to university to study engineering, though a year into the degree, I realised it was not what I wanted to do. So I dropped engineering to focus on history of art. I got my first job in an art gallery in Melbourne, and throughout my twenties I really focused on my art career. I gave lectures at the National Gallery of Victoria, where I noticed that I kept adding funny stories into my lectures.

I was always the clown, and I loved making people laugh. I'd always used humour to get attention in my family. I remember the first time I wrote a comedy sketch was when I was ten, at a camp talent show. I won the contest and continued to write silly plays, songs and sketches throughout high school.

When I was twenty-four, I decided to go on exchange to Glasgow University, which is where I saw an advert for a short course on how to be a stand-up comedian with BBC Scotland. I applied for it, and I had tutorials on how to be a comedian for a couple of hours a week. At the end of that, I had the chance to do five minutes of stand-up – a life-changing moment. My first gig led me to more gigs, and my audiences actually laughed. It was addictive.

I was lying in bed with my son recently, reading a book together, when he turned to me and said, "You are such a good mummy." What I have come to learn is that our children simply need our time. In order to raise happy, confident children, the most important thing is to be there for them always and give them as much time as you can. My favourite mummy moments are as simple as walking to the shops with my children, chatting about anything.

This mad, busy, chaotic motherhood we all seem to embody is crazy. Simply taking moments of calm with our children is all they actually want and need. That's the joy of parenthood.

I'm so excited to raise my daughter in this generation of girls. There are young role models like Jacinda Ardern (the prime minister of New Zealand) and other world leaders, who are simply beacons of kindness, of compassion.

As a family of three, we will often sit and watch old films. My kids will call out the sexism, the racism and all the injustice they see. They question fairness, and they pull me up on it if I ever slip up and rely on stereotypes. I can learn from my children in challenging the past and forging a fairer future for girls.

When I was twenty weeks pregnant with my daughter – my first born – I had that realisation that I've got to really step up and be amazing for her. I knew I had one chance at raising my daughter to be a brilliant strong woman. I wanted to fulfil my dreams, but for her. I wanted to be the best version of me, for her. Having a girl first was a real kick up the ass for me, because I thought, "Right, what am I going to show her?"

My mum was an excellent parent, but she sacrificed her own ambitions to be my dad's support act. Every morning I would wake up to a set breakfast table and a tidy house. My mum put so much effort into supporting our household, but she didn't have the drive to do anything more than that. She was the best stay-at-home-mum, but I knew that wasn't what I wanted to be.

"Success is 80 per cent turning up... Keep trying and you will see a difference."

HELEN THORN

I'm proud that I'm a single parent because it teaches my children that, as a woman, I can put food on the table and support the household, while still doing everything in my career that I want to do. I'm teaching my son, as well as my daughter, that women are just as good as men. Once, a friend said to me, "You aren't a single parent, you're a double parent, because you're doing the work of two!" and I think that's so important. I can provide both role models – of working and parenting – to my children, as one woman.

Here are a few of my top parenting tips:

It's okay to be angry. That may sound silly, but as a people pleaser I'm always wanting others to be happy. I'll be the one to accept the broken biscuit or the smaller piece of cake. When my separation happened, my friends all said, "It's okay to be angry," and I learnt that I don't have to please people all the time. Sometimes working through anger will help you find peace, and I've learnt that I'm allowed to feel all my emotions.

Success is 80 per cent turning up. In any career path, or anything you want to succeed in, the best thing you can do for yourself is to just keep turning up. Keep trying and you will see a difference. In my comedy path, rejection occurs with about 80 per cent of the gigs I want. But it makes those 20 per cent you do get absolutely worth it.

Give children your time. Simply taking moments of calm with our children is all they actually want and need.

Helen's story suggests that to raise resilient girls, we must be resilient parents, something I think Helen has really shown by how she dealt with the tough periods of her life. The concept of resilience can be interpreted in many ways, but I see it as the ability to bounce back from adverse life events. However, there has been significant debate about how to best define, build and measure resilience – particularly in children. Resilience doesn't just appear. It has to be taught over time. I loved hearing what Helen had to say about how she built her resilience over time and now, how she wants to pass on what she has learnt to her daughter.

Resilience is also important for children's mental health. It is widely agreed that children with greater levels of resilience are better able to manage stress, which is a common response to difficult events or adversities. But of course, adversity isn't always avoidable. It's not always possible to prevent parent separation or deaths in families, for example. However, if we work hard to build children's resilience, they will be equipped to better manage life's adversities when they occur.

Helen believes as passionately as I do that now is the time for our girls to rise up. Now is the time for our girls to see fantastic role models. Helen has told me how excited she is about this generation of girls – from Greta Thunberg to Malala Yousafzai, who are almost Joan of Arc characters – and it's through these resilient role models that our girls can see what's possible.

Rise of the Girl

Your daughter might not know this yet, but she's part of a bigger story. Around the world, we see with our own eyes that girls are driving change. From activists who campaign for social and racial equality to influencers who promote positive values – they are rising up. Girls are making their voices heard, and they're calling out for a more equal future. They are leading the way to create a world we all want and that our girls deserve.

The fight for equality goes back more than a hundred years. I hope, like me, you want your daughter, niece, goddaughter or best friend's little girl to grow up and have the opportunity to be a lawyer, sergeant, forensic scientist, astronaut, racing car driver, rugby player, prime minister... or whatever her heart desires. And you want her to get paid the exact same amount for the same work that her male colleagues do. Make sure she knows how hard women have fought over the years and that this is her time to grab every opportunity.

Together, we can raise a new generation of strong, confident young women. Together, we can empower girls and women to realise their inner strengths to dream and do. We recognise the strength in our girls, their creativity and inquisitiveness, and we hear their voice. We must not allow old ways or social obstacles to stop them from reaching their full potential. *Rise of the Girl* is about bringing together a community that can give our girls and young women a supportive environment in which to express their strengths and pursue their ambitions.

My hope with this book is that it will touch the lives of our girls and bring about change for the better. It will be hard to know what progress is being made, and, as always, there's still more challenging work to be done. I go to bed each night wondering if the work I'm doing might change how one girl feels about herself.

What if we could help and guide so many more?

If we want our daughters to reach their full potential, we need to start at home. As parents and caregivers, we have a key role in opening our children's eyes to show them what they're *capable* of. This sometimes feels like an enormous pressure, but we can shape and influence our girls to help them become happy, healthy, capable and confident young women.

Sometimes this starts by showing our girls that we ourselves don't perform strongly all the time, that we're not perfect and we make mistakes too, no matter how old we are. We have to give ourselves and each other permission to stumble and show our daughters how we gently adjust our paths when we do. Because through the stumbles, we learn resilience, courage and personal growth.

The psychologist Erik Erikson spent more than two decades pursuing his interests in human development. He talks about older age being marked by "generativity" – a concern for others and a need to nurture and guide the next generations. We must guide our girls towards finding their purpose. We should show them how to use it to lift themselves up and help them realise that they, in turn, will lift up the next generation beyond them. Perhaps if we can change one girl's future, we can create a chain reaction to help thousands more. Gently remind your girls *never* to underestimate their own power.

Together we rise.

Now is the time for the rise of the girl.

Together we rise.
Now is the time
for the rise of
the girl.

BIBLIOGRAPHY

Foreword

Mueller, C. M. and Dweck, C. S. "Praise for intelligence can undermine children's motivation and performance". *Journal of Personality and Social Psychology*. 1998. https://doi.org/10.1037/0022-3514.75.1.33.

Zamperoni, Victoria. "What new statistics show about children's mental health". 23 November 2018. https://www.mentalhealth.org.uk/blog/what-new-statistics-show-about-childrens-mental-health.

Introduction

Centers for Disease Control and Prevention. "Data and Statistics on Children's Mental Health". Accessed 10 June 2021. https://www.cdc.gov/childrensmentalhealth/data.html.

Fox, Maggie. "Suicides in Teen Girls Hit 40-Year High". 3 August 2017. https://www.nbcnews.com/health/health-news/suicides-teen-girls-hit-40-year-high-n789351.

Girlguiding UK. "A snapshot of girls' and young women's lives". Accessed 10 June 2021. https://www.girlguiding.org.uk/girls-making-change/girls-attitudes-survey.

O'Hagan, Eimear. "Teenage Crisis". 24 June 2018. *Fabulous*. https://www.thescottishsun.co.uk/fabulous/2831282/from-body-issues-to-unprotected-sex-fabulous-speaks-to-six-girls-to-find-out-whats-causing-our-teenage-crisis.

Rocha Rios, Gabrielle. "Girls are Facing a Mental Health Crisis". 29 March 2018. https://www.girlsglobe.org/2018/03/29/girls-facing-mental-health-crisis.

Chapter 1 – Seven

Biddulph, Steve. *Raising Girls in the 21st Century: Helping Our Girls to Grow Up Wise, Strong and Free*. London: Thorsons. 2019.

Chambers, Nick; Elnaz T. Kashefpakdel; Jordan Rehill and Christian Percy. "Drawing the Future". January 2018. https://www.ons.gov.uk/employmentandlabourmarket/peopleinwork/earningsandworkinghours/bulletins/genderpaygapintheuk/2020.

Clark, Nancy F. "Act Now to Shrink the Confidence Gap". 28 April 2014. *Forbes*. https://www.forbes.com/sites/womensmedia/2014/04/28/act-now-to-shrink-the-confidence-gap.

Education.com. "Lucky Age 7: Why and How Kinds Change". 14 May 2014. *Education*. https://www.education.com/magazine/article/Lucky_7_How.

Fraga, Juli. "Do the First 7 Years of Life Really Mean Everything?". 21 December 2017. https://www.healthline.com/health/parenting/first-seven-years-of-childhood.

Goodman, Alissa; Heather Joshi; Bilal Nasim and Claire Tyler.

"Social and emotional skills in childhood and their long-term effects on adult life". 11 March 2015. https://www.eif.org.uk/public/report/social-and-emotional-skills-in-childhood-and-their-long-term-effects-on-adult-life.

Manchester Metropolitan University. "Mentoring and Sponsoring to Generate Routes for Women's Leadership". *GROWL Enquiry Tool*. Accessed 10 June 2021. https://www.mmu.ac.uk/media/mmuacuk/content/documents/business-school/growl/GROWL-A4-Brochure-%E2%80%93-Developing-v2.pdf.

Mohr, Tara Sophia. "Why Women Don't Apply for Jobs Unless They're 100% Qualified". *Harvard Business Review*. 25 August 2014. https://hbr.org/2014/08/why-women-dont-apply-for-jobs-unless-theyre-100-qualified.

National Scientific Council on the Developing Child. "The Science of Early Childhood Development: Closing the Gap Between What We Know and What We Do". 2007. https://developingchild.harvard.edu/resources/the-science-of-early-childhood-development-closing-the-gap-between-what-we-know-and-what-we-do.

Office for National Statistics. "Gender Pay Gap in the UK: 2020". Accessed 10 June 2021. https://www.ons.gov.uk/employmentandlabourmarket/peopleinwork/earningsandworkinghours/bulletins/genderpaygapintheuk/2020.

Chapter 2 – Finding Themselves

Benson, Peter. "Sparks: How Youth Thrive". Filmed May 2010, St Paul, Minnesota. Video. https://www.youtube.com/watch?v=TqzUHcW58Us.

Cherry, Kendra. "Differences of Extrinsic and Intrinsic Motivation". 15 January 2020. https://www.verywellmind.com/differences-between-extrinsic-and-intrinsic-motivation-2795384.

Gardner, H. E. *Frames of Mind: The theory of multiple intelligences.* London: Hachette UK. 2011.

Marenus, Michele. "Gardner's theory of multiple intelligences". *Simply Psychology*. 9 June 2020. https://www.simplypsychology.org/multiple-intelligences.html.

Wen, Tiffanie. "The things that do – and don't – motivate kids to succeed". 5 December 2019. https://www.bbc.com/worklife/article/20191203-the-things-that-do-and-dont-motivate-kids-to-succeed.

Westervelt, Eric. "Q&A: Blocks, Play, Screen Time And The Infant Mind". 21 February 2015. https://www.npr.org/sections/ed/2015/02/12/385264747/q-a-blocks-play-screen-time-and-the-infant-mind?t=1609944643933&t=1623334475019.

Chapter 3 – Empowering Conversations

Conversation 1: "I don't like putting my hand up in class!"

Bian, Lin; Sarah-Jane Leslie and Andrei Cimpian. "Gender

stereotypes about intellectual ability emerge early and influence children's interests". *Science*. 27 January 2017. https://science.sciencemag.org/content/355/6323/389#aff-3.

Chapman, Amanda. "Gender Bias in Education". Accessed 10 June 2021. http://www.edchange.org/multicultural/papers/genderbias.html.

Gunderson, Elizabeth A.; Sarah J. Gripshover et al. "Parent Praise to 1- to 3-Year-Olds Predicts Children's Motivational Frameworks 5 Years Later". *Child Development*. 11 February 2013. https://doi.org/10.1111/cdev.12064.

Ruiz, Don Miguel. *The Four Agreements: Practical Guide to Personal Freedom*. California: Amber-Allen Publishing, Inc., 2018.

Sandberg, Sheryl. "Why we have too few women leaders". Filmed December 2010 at TEDWomen, Washington, DC. Video. https://www.ted.com/talks/sheryl_sandberg_why_we_have_too_few_women_leaders?language=en.

Conversation 2: "I can't do this. Other people do this."

Anxiety & Depression Association of America. "Facts & Statistics". Accessed 10 June 2021. https://adaa.org/understanding-anxiety/facts-statistics.

Center for Collegiate Mental Health. "2020 Annual Report". Accessed 10 June 2021. https://ccmh.memberclicks.net/assets/docs/2020%20CCMH%20Annual%20Report.pdf.

Fowers, Alyssa and William Wan. "A third of Americans now show signs of clinical anxiety or depression, Census Bureau finds amid coronavirus pandemic". *The Washington Post*. 26 May 2020. https://www.washingtonpost.com/health/2020/05/26/americans-with-depression-anxiety-pandemic.

Girlguiding UK. "Mental Health and Guiding". Accessed 10 June 2021. https://www.girlguiding.org.uk/making-guiding-happen/running-your-unit/including-all/including-members-with-additional-needs/mental-health-and-guiding.

Maslow, Abraham H. *Motivation and Personality*. New York: Harper and Row. 1954.

McLeod, Saul A. "Maslow's Hierarchy of Needs". 20 March 2020. *Simply Psychology*. https://www.simplypsychology.org/maslow.html.

Menasce Horowitz, Juliana and Nikki Graf. "Most U.S. Teens See Anxiety and Depression as a Major Problem Among Their Peers". 20 February 2019. https://www.pewresearch.org/social-trends/2019/02/20/most-u-s-teens-see-anxiety-and-depression-as-a-major-problem-among-their-peers.

Snow, Kate and Cynthia McFadden. "Generation at risk: America's youngest facing mental health crisis". 10 December 2017. https://www.nbcnews.com/health/kids-health/generation-risk-america-s-youngest-facing-mental-health-crisis-n827836.

Conversation 3: "I really messed up today – what am I going to do?"

Baycrest Centre for Geriatric Care. "Making mistakes while studying actually helps you learn better". *ScienceDaily*. 11 June 2018. www.sciencedaily.com/releases/2018/06/180611133437.htm.

Cyr, Andrée-Ann and Nicole D. Anderson. "Learning from your mistakes: does it matter if you're out in left foot, I mean field?" *Memory*. 26 October 2018. https://pubmed.ncbi.nlm.nih.gov/29659332.

Espinoza, Javier. "Erasers are an 'instrument of the devil' which should be banned, says academic". *The Telegraph*. 26 May 2015. https://www.telegraph.co.uk/education/educationnews/11630639/Ban-erasers-from-the-classroom-says-academic.html.

Girlguiding UK. "Girls' Attitudes Survey 2020". 2020. https://www.girlguiding.org.uk/globalassets/docs-and-resources/research-and-campaigns/girls-attitudes-survey-2020.pdf.

Gurney Read, Josie. "Lessons in 'grit and resilience' recognised by new award". *The Telegraph*. 7 January 2015. https://www.telegraph.co.uk/education/educationnews/11330877/Lessons-in-grit-and-resilience-recognised-by-new-award.html.

Nielsen, Linda. *Between Fathers and Daughters: Enriching and Rebuilding Your Adult Relationship*. Tennessee: Cumberland House Publishing. 2008.

Nielsen, Linda. *Father-Daughter Relationships: Contemporary Research & Issues*. Oxfordshire: Routledge. 2019.

Nielsen, Linda. "How Dads Affect Their Daughters into Adulthood". 3 June 2014. https://ifstudies.org/blog/how-dads-affect-their-daughters-into-adulthood.

Orth, Ulrich; Richard W. Robins and Keith F. Widaman. "Life-span development of self-esteem and its effects on important life outcomes". *Journal of Personality and Social Psychology*. June 2012. https://pubmed.ncbi.nlm.nih.gov/21942279.

Paul, Caroline. "To raise brave girls, encourage adventure". Filmed December 2016 at TEDWomen, Washington, DC. Video. https://www.ted.com/talks/caroline_paul_to_raise_brave_girls_encourage_adventure.

Roediger, Henry L. and Bridgid Finn. "Getting It Wrong: Surprising Tips on How to Learn". *Scientific American*. 20 October 2009. https://www.scientificamerican.com/article/getting-it-wrong.

Weedy, Simon. "'Risky' UK playgrounds cause a stir across the Atlantic". 16 March 2018. https://www.childinthecity.org/2018/03/16/risky-uk-playgrounds-cause-a-stir-across-the-atlantic.

Conversation 4: "I am rubbish at maths. Even my teacher thinks so!"

Devine, Amy and Kayleigh Fawcett et al. "Gender differences in mathematics anxiety and the relation to mathematics performance while controlling for test anxiety". *Behavioral and Brain Functions.* 9 July 2012. https://doi.org/10.1186/1744-9081-8-33.

Paton, Graeme. "Girls more likely to suffer from 'mathematics anxiety'". *The Telegraph.* 9 July 2012. https://www.telegraph.co.uk/education/educationnews/9385005/Girls-more-likely-to-suffer-from-mathematics-anxiety.html.

Stanford, Peter. "Make Britain Count: Are girls really worse at maths than boys?". *The Telegraph.* 6 March 2012. https://www.telegraph.co.uk/education/maths-reform/9126371/Make-Britain-Count-Are-girls-really-worse-at-maths-than-boys.html.

Strauss, Valerie. "Stop telling kids you're bad at math. You are spreading math anxiety 'like a virus'". *The Washington Post.* 25 April 2016. https://www.washingtonpost.com/news/answer-sheet/wp/2016/04/25/stop-telling-kids-youre-bad-at-math-you-are-spreading-math-anxiety-like-a-virus.

Yousafzai, Malala. Address to United Nations, 12 July 2013. Video. https://www.youtube.com/watch?v=IXxdsb6jT7o.

Conversation 5: "She's really awesome. I wish I could be more like her."

Murden, Fiona. *Mirror Thinking: How Role Models Make Us Human.* London: Bloomsbury Sigma. 2020.

Conversation 6: "Why would she say that? I thought she was my friend."

Caper. "The P.E.A.C.E. Pack". Accessed 12 June 2021. https://www.caper.com.au.

Jacobson, Rae. "Social Media and Self-Doubt". Accessed 12 June 2021. https://childmind.org/article/social-media-and-self-doubt.

Fagell, Phyllis. "Raise girls to be empowered, supportive". *The Journal Gazette.* 1 November 2018. https://www.journalgazette.net/features/20181101/raise-girls-to-be-empowered-supportive.

Kennedy-Moore, Eileen. "Children's Growing Friendships". *Psychology Today.* 26 February 2012. https://www.psychologytoday.com/gb/blog/growing-friendships/201202/childrens-growing-friendships.

Lally, Maria. "Mean Girls: How to talk to your daughter about toxic friendships". *The Telegraph.* 8 April 2016. https://www.telegraph.co.uk/family/parenting/mean-girls-how-to-talk-to-your-daughter-abouttoxic-friendships.

Marinucci, Jeni. "Not fitting in at school: How to help your kid". *Today's Parent.* 15 September 2016. https://www.todaysparent.com/kids/tween-and-teen/not-fitting-in-at-school-how-to-help-your-child.

Plan International USA. "The State of Gender Equality for US Adolescents: Full Research Findings from a National Survey of Adolescents". 12 September 2018. https://www.planusa.org/docs/state-of-gender-equality-2018.pdf.

Conversation 7: "We lost another game. Maybe I should quit."

Andersen, Erika. "21 Quotes From Henry Ford On Business, Leadership And Life". *Forbes*. 31 May 2013. https://www.forbes.com/sites/erikaandersen/2013/05/31/21-quotes-from-henry-ford-on-business-leadership-and-life/?sh=8c3f325293c5.

Goleman, Daniel. *Emotional Intelligence: Why it Can Matter More Than IQ*. London: Bloomsbury. 1996.

Chapter 4 – The Power of Self-Belief

Duckworth, Angela. *Grit: The Power of Passion and Perseverance*. New York: Scribner Book Company. 2016.

Dweck, Carol S. *Mindset: The New Psychology of Success*. New York: Random House. 2006.

Dweck, Carol S. "The Power of Yet". Filmed September 2014 at TEDxNorrkoping, Sweden. Video. https://www.ted.com/talks/carol_dweck_the_power_of_believing_that_you_can_improve.

Kübler-Ross, Elisabeth. *On Death and Dying*. New York: MacMillan. 1969

Mind Tools. "Emotional Intelligence in Leadership". Accessed 12 June 2021. https://www.mindtools.com/pages/article/newLDR_45.htm.

Plan International UK. "The State of Girls' Rights in the UK 2019–2020". 2020. https://www.researchgate.net/profile/Amanda-Ptolomey-2/publication/338750234_Plan_UK_State_of_Girls_Rights%27_in_the_UK_2020/links/5e285bf1a6fdcc70a141e196/Plan-UK-State-of-Girls-Rights-in-the-UK-2020.pdf.

Chapter 5 – Raise Them Resilient

Cherry, Kendra. "Erik Erikson's Stages of Psychosocial Development". 26 June 2020. https://www.verywellmind.com/erik-eriksons-stages-of-psychosocial-development-2795740.

Connley, Courtney. "Michelle Obama shares the No 1 lesson she learned from her mom". 13 May 2018. https://www.cnbc.com/2018/05/11/michelle-obama-shares-the-no-1-lesson-she-learned-from-her-mom.html.

Kay, Katty and Claire Shipman. *The Confidence Code: The Science and Art of Self-Assurance – What Women Should Know*. London: HarperCollins. 2018.

Sandberg, Sheryl. "So we leaned in ... now what?". Filmed December 2013 at TEDWomen, Washington, DC. Video. https://www.ted.com/talks/sheryl_sandberg_so_we_leaned_in_now_what.

Shipman, Claire. "Expert advice for raising confident girls". *Tilted* podcast. 14 November 2018. https://leanin.org/podcast-episodes/expert-advice-for-raising-confident-girls#!

INDEX

ACKNOWLEDGEMENTS

On the fifteenth of May 2019, I was walking across the fields at the back of my house with my three children. It was a lovely, sunny afternoon and we had taken the opportunity to get some fresh air. My youngest at the time was just twelve weeks old and he was strapped to my chest in a baby sling when I received an unexpected phone call. It was my literary agent, Jessica Killingley. She said. "Jo, you know me pretty well and I don't make as many phone calls as you might imagine, but this one seemed important. I'm delighted to say that you've been offered a publishing contract with DK. You did it!"

After the call, I sat on the grass while my two older kids ran around behind me. I paused to take in the enormous news. It was a big day and, in many ways, I was so pleased that it happened when I was able to take in that moment by myself. I sat there with my own thoughts, feeling quite teary, and all I could hear was the sound of my children playing. After three years of creative thoughts, ideas and perseverance, I had finally done it. I had a publishing contract.

I want to use this opportunity to thank all those who have helped and championed me to achieve one of my goals. I have dreamed of writing a book since I was ten years old. So much of what I have achieved in my life would simply not have been possible without the love and steady support of my family and friends.

First and foremost, I want to thank my husband, Lance. He champions me more than anyone else. My partner of more than twenty years and a committed, loving father to our three amazing children. He has always encouraged me to keep going. He has supported me in more ways than one, including taking the kids out for hours on end so I could finish a few chapters. I couldn't ask for more love, laughter, unfailing support and honest feedback.

To my children. My daughter, Erin, for without her, this book may never have been written. She was always my inspiration. From the first moment I held Erin in my arms, I felt so motivated to move towards being my true self – for her. I am so impressed by how she has grown and matured over the last few years. I love watching the person she is becoming. Erin, I am so incredibly proud to be your mum. To my handsome, kind boys, Seth and Nico. You are both a huge source of inspiration for me. Seth, thank you for having such an infectious smile and sense of humour. At times when I was overwhelmed with writing, no one could make me belly laugh like you. Your kind nature and high levels of empathy make me so proud. To Nico, even though you are the youngest, you somehow seem to bring a sense of calm to our chaos. I hope I may have the opportunity to write a book for my boys one day.

To my beloved parents and my brothers, Richard and James, who have been a constant in my life. Your love, support and guidance has gone a long way in shaping the person I have become. Dad, I will always be grateful to you for always reminding me that I was always capable of achieving the things I wanted. You never told me I couldn't do something, just because I was girl. Mum, thank you for your unwavering love and kindness. You are one of the most giving people I know. To my big brother, Richard, it's hard to know where to begin, but you have always been my protector. It has not been easy writing a book around the demands of the business we run together, and I really appreciate your encouragement. I hope that your daughters, Izzy and Jenny, will love this book as much as I do. To my younger brother, James, I will always have the fondest of memories of us as children together. It was through my outdoor adventures with you that I found my own sense of adventure.

To my mother-in-law, Madalene Wimble, who kindly agreed to be a contributor to this book. It was such a pleasure to be able to include your professional and personal thoughts on these pages.

To my lovely sisters-in-law, Camilla and Catherine. You have both always championed my book, which means a tremendous amount to me. Catherine, you will vividly recall me trying to write the outline of my book while our children were doing indoor climbing! I always took my laptop with me on our family holidays – which I know was not always ideal – but thank you for being patient with me.

I also owe a huge debt of appreciation to everyone who has helped me write this book and those who have looked after my children while I wrote. Thank you to Ginny Sutton for caring for the children while I work – you have been a constant source of support. As a working mum of three, I couldn't do what I do without the incredible friendship you have shown to me. To Bethan Sutton, you have been tremendously helpful in typing up the pieces from my contributors, as well as reading through the book for me. To Jazzy Sutton, you have long been a brilliant source of inspiration for my book by helping me understand what is going on in the minds of teenage girls today. I am so appreciative of your patience, love and positive messages.

To all the amazing women in my life: my friends – some of whom I have known for more than thirty years. You all constantly lift me up and I don't think I would be able to function successfully without you all. In no particular order, I would like to thank Sophie, Emma B, Miche R, Linds G, Lucy, Tanya, Emma R, Caz, Erica, Clare, Caroline B, Anna, Julia, Pippa, Claudia, Laura B and Linds P. There are too many to name, but you all have been real rocks of support throughout this process and over the years.

Thank you to all those who helped bring this book to life. A special thanks to Nicky Raby. Without you, I would never have been introduced to my literary agent, Jessica Killingley. A brilliant example of women supporting women, Jessica has been a pillar of support to me in this process and, more than anything, she asked me questions that helped me find clarity on who the book was for, why I was writing it and what I wanted readers to gain from it. They are all simple questions, but – goodness – they are important! Jessica has championed me for my entire book journey and I'm truly grateful to her for her knowledge, expertise and friendship.

To my editor at DK, Stephanie Milner, who took me under her wing as she too believed in the book and in me. I am so grateful to you for seeing the vision for this book and helping me bring it to life. You were one the first people to lay eyes on my manuscript and tell me that you loved it! I will always be grateful to you for your passion and enthusiasm for *Rise of the Girl*. Steph, you are amazing!

I would also like to express my gratitude to Shari Last for editing the book. For the hours we spent trawling through edits. Most of all, you helped me bring the words on the page to life. The time and patience it must take for the editing process is truly commendable. I don't know how you do it! I am so grateful to you for working with me to make every page of this book the best it can be.

Thank you also to Bess Daly for understanding my inspiration to create the illustrations and the look and flow of the book. I really felt a strong connection with you – you just "got" the book from the start. You have created a design that stands so strong and tall on the bookshelves; just like we want every girl to be.

To my contributors, I am so grateful for your valuable wisdom and insight. We know that hearing stories from others, and learning from teachers, mentors, athletes, leaders and entrepreneurs is an inspiring way for girls to expand their creative minds. Piecing all of these stories together has made the book so wonderful. Without the experiences and support from my contributors, Rise of the Girl would, quite simply, not be the amazing book it is. I am so incredibly proud of my contributors, all of whom are supporting our girls to be their best selves. Huge appreciation must be given to all the amazing individuals who have taken the time to contribute to this book. In no particular order, thanks to Rocky Clark, Ruth Cooper-Dickson, Steve Backley, Mark Martin, June Angelides, Jo Jones, Anna Whitehouse, Lorenzo Colangelo, Professor Phillip Slee, Dr Helen Woolnough, Sarah Weller, Michelle Robinson, Madalene Wimble, Nimsdai Purja, Anna Jones, David McQueen, Heidi Petite, Lauren Derrett, Molly Gunn, Philippa Gogarty and Helen Thorn. They have all brought their own thoughts and wisdom to this book, which has made it absolutely brilliant.

Finally, thank you for buying this book. I am so grateful. I hope that for every book that is purchased or passed on to another parent, a conversation may take place that helps support a girl in building her self-confidence or helping her find her passions.